YOU...
H...

VIRGO

YOUR PERSONAL HOROSCOPE 2009

VIRGO

24th August–23rd September

igloo

igloo

This edition published by Igloo Books Ltd,
Cottage Farm, Sywell, Northants NN6 0BJ
www.igloo-books.com

Produced for Igloo Books by W. Foulsham & Co. Ltd,
The Publishing House, Bennetts Close, Cippenham,
Slough, Berkshire SL1 5AP, England

ISBN: 978-1-84817-061-2

Copyright © 2008 W. Foulsham & Co. Ltd

This is an abridged version of material
originally published in *Old Moore's Horoscope
and Astral Diary*.

Printed and manufactured in China

CONTENTS

INTRODUCTION

Your Personal Horoscopes have been specifically created to allow you to get the most from astrological patterns and the way they have a bearing on not only your zodiac sign, but nuances within it. Using the diary section of the book you can read about the influences and possibilities of each and every day of the year. It will be possible for you to see when you are likely to be cheerful and happy or those times when your nature is in retreat and you will be more circumspect. The diary will help to give you a feel for the specific 'cycles' of astrology and the way they can subtly change your day-to-day life. For example, when you see the sign ☿, this means that the planet Mercury is retrograde at that time. Retrograde means it appears to be running backwards through the zodiac. Such a happening has a significant effect on communication skills, but this is only one small aspect of how the Personal Horoscope can help you.

With your Personal Horoscope the story doesn't end with the diary pages. It includes simple ways for you to work out the zodiac sign the Moon occupied at the time of your birth, and what this means for your personality. In addition, if you know the time of day you were born, it is possible to discover your Ascendant, yet another important guide to your personal make-up and potential.

Many readers are interested in relationships and in knowing how well they get on with people of other astrological signs. You might also be interested in the way you appear to very different sorts of individuals. If you are such a person, the section on Venus will be of particular interest. Despite the rapidly changing position of this planet, you can work out your Venus sign, and learn what bearing it will have on your life.

Using Your Personal Horoscope you can travel on one of the most fascinating and rewarding journeys that anyone can take – the journey to a better realisation of self.

THE ESSENCE OF VIRGO

Exploring the Personality of Virgo the Virgin

(24TH AUGUST – 23RD SEPTEMBER)

What's in a sign?

Virgo people tend to be a rather extraordinary sort of mixture. Your ruling planet is Mercury, which makes you inclined to be rather chatty and quite sociable. On the other hand, yours is known as an Earth-ruled zodiac sign, which is usually steady and sometimes quite reserved. Thus, from the start, there are opposing energies ruling your life. This is not a problem when the right sort of balance is achieved and that is what you are looking for all the time. Repressed social and personal communication can make you worrisome, which in turn leads to a slightly fussy tendency that is not your most endearing quality.

At best you are quite ingenious and can usually rely on your strong intuition when weighing up the pros and cons of any given situation. Like all Earth signs you are able to accrue wealth and work hard to achieve your ultimate objectives in life. However, one is left with the impression that problems arise for Virgo when acquisition takes over. In other words you need to relax more and to enjoy the fruits of your successes on a more regular basis.

Tidiness is important to you, and not just around your home. You particularly don't like loose ends and can be meticulous in your sense of detail. It seems likely that the fictional Sherlock Holmes was a Virgo subject and his ability to get to the absolute root of all situations is a stock-in-trade for the sign of the Virgin. Flexibility is especially important in relationships and you shouldn't become so obsessed with the way surroundings look that you fail to make the most of social opportunities.

Another tendency for Virgo is a need to 'keep up with the Joneses'. Why do you do this? Mainly because like your fellow Mercury-ruled sign of Gemini you haven't really as much confidence as seems to be the case. As a result you want to know that you are as good as anyone else, and if possible better. This can, on occasion, lead to a sort of subconscious race that you can never hope to win. Learn to relax, and to recognise when you are on top anyway, and you are really motoring.

Virgo resources

Virgoan people are not at all short of savvy, and one of the most important considerations about your make-up is that you usually know how to proceed in a practical sense. At your disposal you have an armoury of weapons that can lead to a successful sort of life, especially in a practical and financial sense.

Your ruling planet, Mercury, makes you a good communicator and shows you the way to get on-side with the world at large. This quality means that you are rarely short of the right sort of information that is necessary in order to get things right first time. Where this doesn't prove to be possible you have Earth-sign tenacity, and an ability to work extremely hard for long hours in order to achieve your intended objectives. On the way you tend on the whole to make friends, though you might find it hard to get through life without picking up one or two adversaries too.

Virgo people are capable of being gregarious and gossipy, whilst at the same time retaining an internal discipline which more perceptive people are inclined to recognise instinctively. You cement secure friendships and that means nearly always having someone to rely on in times of difficulty. But this isn't a one-way street, because you are a very supportive type yourself and would fight tenaciously on behalf of a person or a cause that you supported wholeheartedly. At such times you can appear to be quite brave, even though you could be quaking inside.

A tendency towards being nervy is not always as evident as you might think, mainly because you have the power and ability to keep it behind closed doors. Retaining the secrets of friends, despite your tendency to indulge in gossip, is an important part of your character and is the reason that others learn to trust you. Organisational skills are good and you love to sort out the puzzles of life, which makes you ideal for tedious jobs that many other people would find impossible to complete. Your curiosity knows no bounds and you would go to almost any length to answer questions that are uppermost in your mind at any point in time.

Beneath the surface

So what are you really like? Well, in the case of Virgo this might be the most interesting journey of all, and one that could deeply surprise even some of those people who think they know you very well indeed. First of all it must be remembered that your ruling planet is Mercury, known as the lord of communication. As a result it's important for you to keep in touch with the world at large. That's fine, except for the fact that your Earth-sign tendencies are inclined to make you basically quiet by nature.

Here we find something of a contradiction and one that leads to more than a few misunderstandings. You are particularly sensitive to little changes out there in the cosmos and so can be much more voluble on some days than on others. The result can be that others see you as being somewhat moody, which isn't really the case at all. You are inclined to be fairly nervy and would rarely be quite as confident as you give the impression of being. Although usually robust in terms of general health, this doesn't always seem to be the case and a tendency towards a slightly hypochondriac nature can be the result. Some Virgoans can make an art form out of believing that they are unwell and you need to understand that part of the reason for this lies in your desire for attention.

Another accusation that is levelled at Virgoans is that they are inclined to be fussy over details. This is also an expression of your lack of basic confidence in yourself. For some reason you subconsciously assume that if every last matter is dealt with absolutely, all will work out well. In reality the more relaxed you remain, the better you find your ability to cope with everyday life. The simple truth is that you are much more capable than your inner nature tends to believe and could easily think more of yourself than you do. You have a logical mind, but also gain from the intuition that is possessed by all Mercury-ruled individuals. The more instinctive you become, the less you worry about things and the more relaxed life can seem to be. You also need to override a natural suspicion of those around you. Trust is a hard thing for you, but a very important one.

Making the best of yourself

There are many ways in which you can exploit the best potentials of your zodiac sign, and at the same time play down some of the less favourable possibilities. From the very start it's important to realise that the main criticism that comes your way from the outside world is that you are too fussy by half. So, simply avoid being critical of others and the way they do things. By all means stick to your own opinions, but avoid forcing them onto other people. If you can get over this hurdle, your personal popularity will already be that much greater. If people love you, you care for them in return – it's as simple as that, because at heart you aren't really very complicated.

Despite the fact that a little humility would go a long way, you also do need to remain sure of yourself. There's no real problem in allowing others their head, while following your own opinions all the same. Use your practical skills to the full and don't rush things just because other people seem to do so. Although you are ruled by quick Mercury you also come from an Earth sign, which means steady progress.

Find outlets to desensitise your over-nervy nature. You can do this with plenty of healthy exercise and by taking an interest in subject matter that isn't of any great importance, but which you find appealing all the same. Avoid concentrating too much on any one thing, because that is the road to paranoia.

Realise that you have an innate sense of what is right, and that if it is utilised in the right way you can make gains for yourself and for the people you love. You have a good fund of ideas, so don't be afraid to use them. Most important of all you need to remain confident but flexible. That's the path to popularity – something you need much more than you might realise.

The impressions you give

This can be something of a problem area to at least some people born under the zodiac sign of Virgo. There isn't much doubt that your heart is in the right place and this fact isn't lost on many observers. All the same, you can appear to be very definite in your opinions, in fact to the point of stubbornness, and you won't give ground when you know you are in the right. A slight problem here might be that Virgoans nearly always think they have the moral and legal high ground. In the majority of cases this may indeed be true, but there are ways and means of putting the message across.

What Virgo needs more than anything else is tact. A combination of Mercury, ruling your means of communication, and your Earth-sign heritage can, on occasions, make you appear to be rather blunt. Mercury also aids in quick thinking and problem solving. The sum total can make it appear that you don't take other people's opinions into account and that you are prepared to railroad your ideas through if necessary.

Most people recognise that you are very capable, and may therefore automatically turn to you for leadership. It isn't certain how you will react under any given circumstance because although you can criticise others, your Earth-sign proclivities don't make you a natural leader. In a strong supportive role you can be wonderful and it is towards this scenario that you might choose to look.

Avoid people accusing you of being fussy by deliberately cultivating flexibility in your thinking and your actions. You are one of the kindest and most capable people to be found anywhere in the zodiac. All you need to do to complete the picture is to let the world at large know what you are. With your natural kindness and your ability to get things done you can show yourself to be a really attractive individual. Look towards a brush-up of your public persona. Deep inside you are organised and caring, though a little nervy. Let people know exactly what you are – it only makes you more human.

The way forward

Before anyone can move forward into anything it is important for them to realise exactly where they are now. In your case this is especially true. Probably the most problematic area of Virgo is in realising not what is being done but rather why. It is the inability to ask this question on a regular basis that leads Virgo into a rut now and again. Habit isn't simply a word to many people born under the zodiac sign of Virgo, it's a religion. The strange thing about this fact is that if you find yourself catapulted, against your will, into a different sort of routine, you soon learn to adopt it as if it were second nature. In other words this way of behaving is endemic, but not necessarily inevitable. The way out of it is simple and comes thanks to your ruling planet of Mercury. Keep talking, and at the same time listen. Adapt your life on a regular basis and say 'So many habits are not necessary' at least ten times a day.

All the same it wouldn't be very prudent to throw out the baby with the bath water. Your ability to stick at things is justifiably legendary. This generally means that you arrive at your desired destination in life, even though it might take you a long time to get there. The usual result is respect from people who don't have your persistence or tenacity.

With regard to love and affection you are in a good position to place a protecting blanket around those you love the most. This is fine, as long as you check regularly that you are not suffocating them with it. If you allow a certain degree of freedom people will respect your concern all the more, and they won't fight against it. By all means communicate your affection and don't allow your natural Earth-sign reserve to get in the way of expressing feelings that are quite definite internally. This is another aspect of letting the world know what you are really like and is of crucial importance to your zodiac sign.

You need variety, and if possible an absence of worry. Only when things are going wrong do Virgoans become the fussy individuals that sometimes attract a little criticism. As long as you feel that you are in charge of your own destiny, you can remain optimistic – another vital requisite for Virgo. With just a little effort you can be one of the most popular and loved people around. Add to this your natural ability to succeed and the prognosis for the sign of the Virgin is very good.

VIRGO ON THE CUSP

Astrological profiles are altered for those people born at either the beginning or the end of a zodiac sign, or, more properly, on the cusps of a sign. In the case of Leo this would be on the 24th of August and for two or three days after, and similarly at the end of the sign, probably from the 21st to the 23rd of September.

The Leo Cusp – August 24th to 26th

If anything is designed to lighten the load of being a Virgoan, it's having a Leo quality in the nature too. All Virgoans are inclined to take themselves too seriously on occasions and they don't have half as much self-esteem as they could really use effectively. Being born on the Leo cusp gives better self-confidence, less of the supreme depths which Virgo alone can display and a much more superficial view of many aspects of life. The material success for which Virgo is famous probably won't be lacking, but there will also be a determination to have fun and let the bright, aspiring qualities that are so popular in the Leo character show.

In matters of love, you are likely to be easy-going, bright, bubbly and always willing to have a laugh. You relish good company, and though you sometimes go at things like a bull at a gate, your intentions are true and you know how to get others to like you a great deal. Family matters are right up your street, because not only do you have the ability to put down firm and enduring roots, but you are the most staunch and loyal protector of family values that anyone could wish for.

When it comes to working, you seem to have the best combination of all. You have the ability to work long and hard, achieving your objectives as all Virgoans do, but managing to do so with a smile permanently fixed to your face. You are naturally likely to find yourself at the head of things, where your combination of skills is going to be of the greatest use. This sign combination is to be found in every nook and cranny of the working world but perhaps less frequently in jobs which involve getting your hands dirty.

There are times when you definitely live on your nerves and when you don't get the genuine relaxation that the Virgoan qualities within you demand. Chances are you are much more robust than you consider yourself to be, and as long as you keep busy most of the time you tend to enjoy a contented life. The balance usually works well, because Leo lifts Virgo, whilst Virgo stabilises an often too superficial Lion.

The Libra Cusp – September 21st to 23rd

Virgo responds well to input from other parts of the zodiac and probably never more so than in the case of the Libran cusp. The reasons for this are very simple: what Virgo on its own lacks, Libra possesses, and it's the same on the other side of the coin. Libra is often flighty and doesn't take enough time to rest, but it is compensated by the balance inherent in the sign, so it weighs things carefully. Virgo on the other hand is deep and sometimes dark, but because it's ruled by capricious little Mercury, it can also be rather too impetuous. The potential break-even point is obvious and usually leads to a fairly easy-going individual, who is intellectual, thoughtful and practical when necessary.

You are a great person to have around in good times and bad, and you know how to have fun. A staunch support and helper to your friends, you enjoy a high degree of popularity, which usually extends to affairs of the heart. There may be more than one of these in your life and it's best for people born on this cusp not to marry in haste or too early in life. But even if you get things wrong first time around, you have the ability to bounce back quickly and don't become easily discouraged. It is good for you to be often in the company of gregarious and interesting people, but you are quite capable of surviving on your own when you have to.

Health matters may be on your mind more than is strictly necessary, and it's true that you can sometimes worry yourself into minor ailments that would not otherwise have existed. It is important for you to get plenty of rest and also to enjoy yourself. The more you work on behalf of others, the less time you spend thinking about your own possible ailments. Anxiety needs to be avoided, often by getting to the root of a problem and solving it quickly.

A capable and committed worker, you are at your best when able to share the decisions, but you are quite reliable when you have to make up your mind alone. You would never bully those beneath you. You are never short of support and you bring joy to life most of the time.

VIRGO AND ITS ASCENDANTS

The nature of every individual on the planet is composed of the rich variety of zodiac signs and planetary positions that were present at the time of their birth. Your Sun sign, which in your case is Virgo, is one of the many factors when it comes to assessing the unique person you are. Probably the most important consideration, other than your Sun sign, is to establish the zodiac sign that was rising over the eastern horizon at the time that you were born. This is your Ascending or Rising sign. Most popular astrology fails to take account of the Ascendant, and yet its importance remains with you from the very moment of your birth, through every day of your life. The Ascendant is evident in the way you approach the world, and so, when meeting a person for the first time, it is this astrological influence that you are most likely to notice first. Our Ascending sign essentially represents what we appear to be, while the Sun sign is what we feel inside ourselves.

The Ascendant also has the potential for modifying our overall nature. For example, if you were born at a time of day when Virgo was passing over the eastern horizon (this would be around the time of dawn) then you would be classed as a double Virgo. As such, you would typify this zodiac sign, both internally and in your dealings with others. However, if your Ascendant sign turned out to be a Fire sign, such as Aries, there would be a profound alteration of nature, away from the expected qualities of Virgo.

One of the reasons why popular astrology often ignores the Ascendant is that it has always been rather difficult to establish. We have found a way to make this possible by devising an easy-to-use table, which you will find on page 157 of this book. Using this, you can establish your Ascendant sign at a glance. You will need to know your rough time of birth, then it is simply a case of following the instructions.

For those readers who have no idea of their time of birth it might be worth allowing a good friend, or perhaps your partner, to read through the section that follows this introduction. Someone who deals with you on a regular basis may easily discover your Ascending sign, even though you could have some difficulty establishing it for yourself. A good understanding of this component of your nature is essential if you want to be aware of that 'other person' who is responsible for the way you make contact with the world at large. Your Sun sign, Ascendant sign, and the other pointers in this book will, together, allow you a far better understanding of what makes you tick as an individual. Peeling back the different layers of your astrological make-up can be an enlightening experience, and the Ascendant may represent one of the most important layers of all.

Virgo with Virgo Ascendant

You get the best of both worlds, and on rare occasions the worst too. Frighteningly efficient, you have the ability to scare people with your constant knack of getting it right. This won't endear you to everyone, particularly those who pride themselves on being disorganised. You make a loyal friend and would do almost anything for someone who is important to you, though you do so in a quiet way because you are not the most noisy of types. Chances are that you possess the ability to write well and you also have a cultured means of verbal communication on those occasions when you really choose to speak out.

It isn't difficult for you to argue your case, though much of the time you refuse to do so and can lock yourself into your own private world for days on end. If you are at ease with yourself you possess a powerful personality, which you can express well. Conversely, you can live on your nerves and cause problems for yourself. Meditation is good, fussing over details that really don't matter at all is less useful. Once you have chosen a particular course of action there are few people around with sufficient will-power to prevent you from getting what you want. Wide open spaces where the hand of nature is all around can make you feel very relaxed.

Virgo with Libra Ascendant

Libra has the ability to lighten almost any load and it is particularly good at doing so when it is brought together with the much more repressed sign of Virgo. To the world at large you seem relaxed, happy and able to cope with most of the pressures that life places upon you. Not only do you deal with your own life in a bright and breezy manner but you are usually on hand to help others out of any dilemma that they might make for themselves. With excellent powers of communication you leave the world at large in no doubt whatsoever concerning both your opinions and your wishes. It is in the talking stakes that you really excel because Virgo brings the silver tongue of Mercury and Libra adds the Air-sign desire to be in constant touch with the world outside your door.

You like to have a good time and are often found in the company of interesting and stimulating people, who have the ability to bring out the very best in your bright and sparkling personality. Underneath however, there is still much of the worrying Virgoan to be found and this means that you have to learn to relax inside as well as appearing to do so externally. In fact you are much more complex than most people would realise and definitely would not be suited to a life that allowed you too much time to think about yourself.

Virgo with Scorpio Ascendant

This is intensity carried through to the absolute. If you have a problem it is that you fail to externalise all that is going on inside that deep, bubbling cauldron of your inner self. Realising what you are capable of is not a problem, these only start when you have to make it plain to those around you what you want. Part of the reason for this is that you don't always understand yourself. You love intensely and would do absolutely anything for a person you are fond of, even though you might have to inconvenience yourself a great deal on the way. Relationships can cause you slight problems however, since you need to associate with people who at least come somewhere near to understanding what makes you tick. If you manage to bridge the gap between yourself and the world that constantly knocks on your door, you show yourself to be powerful, magnetic and compulsive.

There are times when you definitely prefer to stay quiet though you do have a powerful ability to get your message across when you think it is necessary to do so. There are people around who might think that you are a push-over but they could easily get a shock when you sense that the time is right to answer back. You probably have a very orderly house and don't care for clutter of any sort.

Virgo with Sagittarius Ascendant

This is a combination that might look rather odd at first sight because these two signs have so very little in common. However the saying goes that opposites attract and in terms of the personality you display to the world this is especially true in your case. Not everyone understands what makes you tick but you try to show the least complicated face to the world that you can manage to display. You can be deep and secretive on occasions, and yet at other times you can start talking as soon as you climb out of bed and never stop until you are back there again. Inspirational and spontaneous, you take the world by storm on those occasions when you are free from worries and firing on all cylinders. It is a fact that you support your friends, though there are rather more of them than would be the case for Virgo taken on its own and you don't always choose them as wisely as you might.

There are times when you display a temper and although Sagittarius is incapable of bearing a grudge, the same cannot be said for Virgo, which has a better memory than the elephant. For the best results in life you need to relax as much as possible and avoid overheating that powerful and busy brain. Virgo gives you the ability to concentrate on one thing at once, a skill you should encourage.

Virgo with Capricorn Ascendant

Your endurance, persistence and concentration are legendary and there is virtually nothing that eludes you once you have the bit between your teeth. You are not the pushy, fussy, go-getting sort of Virgoan but are steady, methodical and very careful. Once you have made up your mind, a whole team of wild horses could not change it and although this can be a distinct blessing at times, it is a quality that can bring odd problems into your life too. The difficulty starts when you adopt a lost or less than sensible cause. Even in the face of overwhelming evidence that you are wrong there is something inside you that prevents any sort of U-turn and so you walk forward as solidly as only you are able, to a destination that won't suit you at all.

There are few people around who are more loyal and constant than you can be. There is a lighter and brighter side to your nature and the one or two people who are most important in your life will know how to bring it out. You have a wicked sense of humour, particularly if you have had a drink or when you are feeling on top form. Travel does you the world of good, even if there is a part of you that would rather stay at home. You have a potent, powerful and magnetic personality but for much of the time it is kept carefully hidden.

Virgo with Aquarius Ascendant

How could anyone make convention unconventional? Well, if anyone can manage, you can. There are great contradictions here because on the one hand you always want to do what is expected, but the Aquarian quality within your nature loves to surprise everyone on the way. If you don't always know what you are thinking or doing, it's a pretty safe bet that others won't either, so it's important on occasions to stop and really think. However this is not a pressing concern because you tend to live a fairly happy life and muddle through no matter what. Other people tend to take to you well and it is likely that you will have many friends. You tend to be bright and cheerful and can approach even difficult tasks with the certainty that you have the skills necessary to see them through to their conclusion. Give and take are important factors in the life of any individual and particularly so in your case. Because you can stretch yourself in order to understand what makes other people think and act in the way that they do, you have the reputation of being a good friend and a reliable colleague.

In love you can be somewhat more fickle than the typical Virgoan and yet you are always interesting to live with. Where you are, things happen, and you mix a sparkling wit with deep insights.

Virgo with Pisces Ascendant

You might have been accused on occasions of being too sensitive for your own good, a charge that is not entirely without foundation. Certainly you are very understanding of the needs of others, sometimes to the extent that you put everything aside to help them. This would also be true in the case of charities, for you care very much about the world and the people who cling tenaciously to its surface. Your ability to love on a one-to-one basis knows no bounds though you may not discriminate as much as you could, particularly when young, and might have one or two false starts in the love stakes. You don't always choose to verbalise your thoughts and this can cause problems, because there is always so much going on in your mind and Virgo especially needs good powers of communication. Pisces is quieter and you need to force yourself to say what you think when the explanation is important.

You would never betray a confidence and sometimes take on rather more for the sake of your friends than is strictly good for you. This is not a fault but can cause you problems all the same. Because you are so intuitive there is little that escapes your attention, though you should avoid being pessimistic about your insights. Changes of scenery suit you and extensive travel would bring out the best in what can be a repressed nature at times.

Virgo with Aries Ascendant

Virgo is steady and sure, though also fussy and stubborn. Aries is fast and determined, restless and active. It can be seen already that this is a rather strange meeting of characteristics and because Virgo is ruled by capricious Mercury, the result will change from hour to hour and day to day. It isn't merely that others find it difficult to know where they are with you; they can't even understand what makes you tick. This will make you the subject of endless fascination and attention, at which you will be apparently surprised but inwardly pleased. If anyone ever really gets to know what goes on in that busy mind they may find the implications very difficult to deal with and it is a fact that only you would have the ability to live inside your crowded head.

As a partner and a parent you are second to none, though you would tend to get on better with your children once they started to grow, since by this time you may be slightly less restricting to their own desires, which will often clash with your own on their behalf. You are capable of give and take and could certainly not be considered selfish, though your desire to get the best from everyone might be misconstrued on occasion.

Virgo with Taurus Ascendant

This combination tends to amplify the Taurean qualities that you naturally possess and this is the case because both Taurus and Virgo are Earth signs. However, there are certain factors related to Virgo that show themselves very differently than the sign's cousin Taurus. Virgo is more fussy, nervy and pedantic than Taurus and all of these qualities are going to show up in your nature at one level or another. On the plus side you might be slightly less concerned about having a perfect home and a perfect family, and your interest in life appears at a more direct level than that of the true Taurean. You care very much about your home and family and are very loyal to your friends. It's true that you sometimes tend to try and take them over and you can also show a marked tendency to dominate, but your heart is in the right place and most people recognise that your caring is genuine.

One problem is that there are very few shades of grey in your life, which is certainly not the case for other zodiac sign combinations. Living your life in the way that you do there isn't much room for compromise and this fact alone can prove to be something of a problem where relationships are concerned. In a personal sense you need a partner who is willing to be organised and one who relies on your judgements, which don't change all that often.

Virgo with Gemini Ascendant

A Gemini Ascendant means that you are ruled by Mercury, both through your Sun sign and through the sign that was rising at the time of your birth. This means that words are your basic tools in life and you use them to the full. Some writers have this combination, because even speaking to people virtually all the time is not enough. Although you have many friends you are fairly high-minded, which means that you can make enemies too. The fact is that people either care very much for you, or else they don't like you at all. This can be difficult for you to come to terms with because you don't really set out to cause friction – it simply attracts itself to you.

Although you love travel, home is important too and there is a basic insecurity in your nature that comes about as a result of an overdose of Mercury, which makes you nervy and sometimes far less confident than anyone would guess. Success in your life may be slower arriving with this combination because you are determined to achieve your objectives on your own terms and this can take time. Always a contradiction, often a puzzle to others, your ultimate happiness in life is directly proportional to the effort you put in, though this should not mean wearing yourself out on the way.

Virgo with Cancer Ascendant

What can this union of zodiac signs bring to the party that isn't there in either Virgo or Cancer alone? Well quite a bit actually. Virgo can be very fussy on occasions and too careful for its own good. The presence of steady, serene Cancer alters the perspectives and allows a smoother, more flowing Virgoan to greet the world. You are chatty, easy to know and exhibit a combination of the practical skills of Virgo, together with the deep and penetrating insights that are typical of Cancer. This can make you appear to be very powerful, and your insights are second to none. You are a born organiser and love to be where things are happening, even if you are only there to help make the sandwiches or to pour the tea. Invariably your role will be much greater but you don't seek personal acclaim and are a good team player on most occasions.

There is a quiet side to your nature and those who live with you will eventually get used to your need for solitude. This seems strange because Virgo is generally such a chatterbox and, taken on its own, is rarely quiet for long. In love you show great affection and a sense of responsibility that makes you an ideal parent, though it is possible sometimes that you care rather more than you are willing to show.

Virgo with Leo Ascendant

Here we have cheerfulness allied to efficiency, which can be a very positive combination most of the time. With all the sense of honour, justice and bravery of the Leo subject, Virgo adds staying power through tedious situations and offers you a slightly more serious view of life than we would expect from the Lion alone. In almost any situation you can keep going until you get to your chosen destination and you also find the time to reach out to the people who need your unique nature the most. Few would deny your kindness, though you can attract a little envy because it seems as though yours is the sort of personality that everyone else wants.

Most people born with this combination have a radiant smile and will do their best to think situations through carefully. If there is a tendency to be foolhardy, it is carefully masked beneath a covering of Virgoan common sense. Family matters are dealt with efficiently and with great love. Some might see you as close one moment and distant the next. The truth is that you are always on the go and have a thousand different things to think about, all at the same time. On the whole your presence is noticed and you may represent the most loyal friend of them all.

THE MOON AND THE PART IT PLAYS IN YOUR LIFE

In astrology the Moon is probably the single most important heavenly body after the Sun. Its unique position, as partner to the Earth on its journey around the solar system, means that the Moon appears to pass through the signs of the zodiac extremely quickly. The zodiac position of the Moon at the time of your birth plays a great part in personal character and is especially significant in the build-up of your emotional nature.

Your Own Moon Sign

Discovering the position of the Moon at the time of your birth has always been notoriously difficult because tracking the complex zodiac positions of the Moon is not easy. This process has been reduced to three simple stages with our Lunar Tables. A breakdown of the Moon's zodiac positions can be found from page 35 onwards, so that once you know what your Moon Sign is, you can see what part this plays in the overall build-up of your personal character.

If you follow the instructions on the next page you will soon be able to work out exactly what zodiac sign the Moon occupied on the day that you were born and you can then go on to compare the reading for this position with those of your Sun sign and your Ascendant. It is partly the comparison between these three important positions that goes towards making you the unique individual you are.

HOW TO DISCOVER YOUR MOON SIGN

This is a three-stage process. You may need a pen and a piece of paper but if you follow the instructions below the process should only take a minute or so.

STAGE 1 First of all you need to know the Moon Age at the time of your birth. If you look at Moon Table 1, on page 33, you will find all the years between 1911 and 2009 down the left side. Find the year of your birth and then trace across to the right to the month of your birth. Where the two intersect you will find a number. This is the date of the New Moon in the month that you were born. You now need to count forward the number of days between the New Moon and your own birthday. For example, if the New Moon in the month of your birth was shown as being the 6th and you were born on the 20th, your Moon Age Day would be 14. If the New Moon in the month of your birth came after your birthday, you need to count forward from the New Moon in the previous month. If you were born in a Leap Year, remember to count the 29th February. You can tell if your birth year was a Leap Year if the last two digits can be divided by four. Whatever the result, jot this number down so that you do not forget it.

STAGE 2 Take a look at Moon Table 2 on page 34. Down the left hand column look for the date of your birth. Now trace across to the month of your birth. Where the two meet you will find a letter. Copy this letter down alongside your Moon Age Day.

STAGE 3 Moon Table 3 on page 34 will supply you with the zodiac sign the Moon occupied on the day of your birth. Look for your Moon Age Day down the left hand column and then for the letter you found in Stage 2. Where the two converge you will find a zodiac sign and this is the sign occupied by the Moon on the day that you were born.

Your Zodiac Moon Sign Explained

You will find a profile of all zodiac Moon Signs on pages 35 to 38, showing in yet another way how astrology helps to make you into the individual that you are. In each daily entry of the Astral Diary you can find the zodiac position of the Moon for every day of the year. This also allows you to discover your lunar birthdays. Since the Moon passes through all the signs of the zodiac in about a month, you can expect something like twelve lunar birthdays each year. At these times you are likely to be emotionally steady and able to make the sort of decisions that have real, lasting value.

MOON TABLE 1

YEAR	JUL	AUG	SEP	YEAR	JUL	AUG	SEP	YEAR	JUL	AUG	SEP
1911	25	24	22	1944	20	18	17	1977	16	14	13
1912	15	13	12	1945	9	8	6	1978	5	4	2
1913	3	2/31	30	1946	28	26	25	1979	24	22	21
1914	22	21	19	1947	17	16	14	1980	12	11	10
1915	11	10	9	1948	6	5	3	1981	1/31	29	28
1916	30	29	27	1949	25	24	23	1982	20	19	17
1917	18	17	15	1950	15	13	12	1983	10	8	7
1918	8	6	4	1951	4	2	1	1984	28	26	25
1919	27	25	23	1952	23	20	19	1985	17	16	14
1920	15	14	12	1953	11	9	8	1986	7	5	4
1921	5	3	2	1954	29	28	27	1987	25	24	23
1922	24	22	21	1955	19	17	16	1988	13	12	11
1923	14	12	10	1956	8	6	4	1989	3	1/31	29
1924	2/31	30	28	1957	27	25	23	1990	22	20	19
1925	20	19	18	1958	16	15	13	1991	11	9	8
1926	9	8	7	1959	6	4	3	1992	29	28	26
1927	28	27	25	1960	24	22	21	1993	19	17	16
1928	17	16	14	1961	12	11	10	1994	8	7	5
1929	6	5	3	1962	1/31	30	28	1995	27	26	24
1930	25	24	22	1963	20	19	17	1996	15	14	13
1931	15	13	12	1964	9	7	6	1997	4	3	2
1932	3	2/31	30	1965	28	26	25	1998	23	22	20
1933	22	21	19	1966	17	16	14	1999	13	11	10
1934	11	10	9	1967	7	5	4	2000	1/31	29	27
1935	30	29	27	1968	25	24	23	2001	20	19	17
1936	18	17	15	1969	13	12	11	2002	9	8	6
1937	8	6	4	1970	4	2	1	2003	28	27	26
1938	27	25	23	1971	22	20	19	2004	16	14	13
1939	16	15	13	1972	11	9	8	2005	6	4	3
1940	5	4	2	1973	29	28	27	2006	25	23	22
1941	24	22	21	1974	19	17	16	2007	15	13	12
1942	13	12	10	1975	9	7	5	2008	31	31	30
1943	2	1/30	29	1976	27	25	23	2009	22	20	19

TABLE 2

DAY	AUG	SEP
1	U	X
2	U	X
3	V	X
4	V	Y
5	V	Y
6	V	Y
7	V	Y
8	V	Y
9	V	Y
10	V	Y
11	V	Y
12	V	Y
13	V	Y
14	W	Z
15	W	Z
16	W	Z
17	W	Z
18	W	Z
19	W	Z
20	W	Z
21	W	Z
22	W	Z
23	W	Z
24	X	a
25	X	a
26	X	a
27	X	a
28	X	a
29	X	a
30	X	a
31	X	–

MOON TABLE 3

M/D	U	V	W	X	Y	Z	a
0	LE	LE	LE	VI	VI	LI	LI
1	LE	VI	VI	VI	LI	LI	LI
2	VI	VI	VI	LI	LI	LI	LI
3	VI	VI	LI	LI	LI	SC	SC
4	LI	LI	LI	LI	SC	SC	SC
5	LI	LI	SC	SC	SC	SC	SA
6	LI	SC	SC	SC	SA	SA	SA
7	SC	SC	SA	SA	SA	SA	SA
8	SC	SC	SA	SA	SA	CP	CP
9	SA	SA	SA	SA	CP	CP	CP
10	SA	SA	CP	CP	CP	CP	AQ
11	CP	CP	CP	CP	AQ	AQ	AQ
12	CP	CP	AQ	AQ	AQ	AQ	PI
13	CP	CP	AQ	AQ	AQ	PI	PI
14	AQ	AQ	PI	PI	PI	PI	AR
15	AQ	AQ	PI	PI	PI	PI	AR
16	AQ	PI	PI	PI	AR	AR	AR
17	PI	PI	PI	AR	AR	AR	AR
18	PI	PI	AR	AR	AR	AR	TA
19	PI	AR	AR	AR	TA	TA	TA
20	AR	AR	TA	TA	TA	TA	GE
21	AR	TA	TA	TA	GE	GE	GE
22	TA	TA	TA	GE	GE	GE	GE
23	TA	TA	GE	GE	GE	GE	CA
24	TA	GE	GE	GE	CA	CA	CA
25	GE	GE	CA	CA	CA	CA	CA
26	GE	CA	CA	CA	LE	LE	LE
27	CA	CA	CA	LE	LE	LE	LE
28	CA	CA	LE	LE	LE	LE	VI
29	CA	LE	LE	LE	VI	VI	VI

AR = Aries, TA = Taurus, GE = Gemini, CA = Cancer, LE = Leo, VI = Virgo, LI = Libra, SC = Scorpio, SA = Sagittarius, CP = Capricorn, AQ = Aquarius, PI = Pisces

MOON SIGNS

Moon in Aries

You have a strong imagination, courage, determination and a desire to do things in your own way and forge your own path through life.

Originality is a key attribute; you are seldom stuck for ideas although your mind is changeable and you could take the time to focus on individual tasks. Often quick-tempered, you take orders from few people and live life at a fast pace. Avoid health problems by taking regular time out for rest and relaxation.

Emotionally, it is important that you talk to those you are closest to and work out your true feelings. Once you discover that people are there to help, there is less necessity for you to do everything yourself.

Moon in Taurus

The Moon in Taurus gives you a courteous and friendly manner, which means you are likely to have many friends.

The good things in life mean a lot to you, as Taurus is an Earth sign that delights in experiences which please the senses. Hence you are probably a lover of good food and drink, which may in turn mean you need to keep an eye on the bathroom scales, especially as looking good is also important to you.

Emotionally you are fairly stable and you stick by your own standards. Taureans do not respond well to change. Intuition also plays an important part in your life.

Moon in Gemini

You have a warm-hearted character, sympathetic and eager to help others. At times reserved, you can also be articulate and chatty: this is part of the paradox of Gemini, which always brings duplicity to the nature. You are interested in current affairs, have a good intellect, and are good company and likely to have many friends. Most of your friends have a high opinion of you and would be ready to defend you should the need arise. However, this is usually unnecessary, as you are quite capable of defending yourself in any verbal confrontation.

Travel is important to your inquisitive mind and you find intellectual stimulus in mixing with people from different cultures. You also gain much from reading, writing and the arts but you do need plenty of rest and relaxation in order to avoid fatigue.

Moon in Cancer

The Moon in Cancer at the time of birth is a fortunate position as Cancer is the Moon's natural home. This means that the qualities of compassion and understanding given by the Moon are especially enhanced in your nature, and you are friendly and sociable and cope well with emotional pressures. You cherish home and family life, and happily do the domestic tasks. Your surroundings are important to you and you hate squalor and filth. You are likely to have a love of music and poetry.

Your basic character, although at times changeable like the Moon itself, depends on symmetry. You aim to make your surroundings comfortable and harmonious, for yourself and those close to you.

Moon in Leo

The best qualities of the Moon and Leo come together to make you warm-hearted, fair, ambitious and self-confident. With good organisational abilities, you invariably rise to a position of responsibility in your chosen career. This is fortunate as you don't enjoy being an 'also-ran' and would rather be an important part of a small organisation than a menial in a large one.

You should be lucky in love, and happy, provided you put in the effort to make a comfortable home for yourself and those close to you. It is likely that you will have a love of pleasure, sport, music and literature. Life brings you many rewards, most of them as a direct result of your own efforts, although you may be luckier than average and ready to make the best of any situation.

Moon in Virgo

You are endowed with good mental abilities and a keen receptive memory, but you are never ostentatious or pretentious. Naturally quite reserved, you still have many friends, especially of the opposite sex. Marital relationships must be discussed carefully and worked at so that they remain harmonious, as personal attachments can be a problem if you do not give them your full attention.

Talented and persevering, you possess artistic qualities and are a good homemaker. Earning your honours through genuine merit, you work long and hard towards your objectives but show little pride in your achievements. Many short journeys will be undertaken in your life.

Moon in Libra

With the Moon in Libra you are naturally popular and make friends easily. People like you, probably more than you realise, you bring fun to a party and are a natural diplomat. For all its good points, Libra is not the most stable of astrological signs and, as a result, your emotions can be a little unstable too. Therefore, although the Moon in Libra is said to be good for love and marriage, your Sun sign and Rising sign will have an important effect on your emotional and loving qualities.

You must remember to relate to others in your decision-making. Co-operation is crucial because Libra represents the 'balance' of life that can only be achieved through harmonious relationships. Conformity is not easy for you because Libra, an Air sign, likes its independence.

Moon in Scorpio

Some people might call you pushy. In fact, all you really want to do is to live life to the full and protect yourself and your family from the pressures of life. Take care to avoid giving the impression of being sarcastic or impulsive and use your energies wisely and constructively.

You have great courage and you invariably achieve your goals by force of personality and sheer effort. You are fond of mystery and are good at predicting the outcome of situations and events. Travel experiences can be beneficial to you.

You may experience problems if you do not take time to examine your motives in a relationship, and also if you allow jealousy, always a feature of Scorpio, to cloud your judgement.

Moon in Sagittarius

The Moon in Sagittarius helps to make you a generous individual with humanitarian qualities and a kind heart. Restlessness may be intrinsic as your mind is seldom still. Perhaps because of this, you have a need for change that could lead you to several major moves during your adult life. You are not afraid to stand your ground when you know your judgement is right, you speak directly and have good intuition.

At work you are quick, efficient and versatile and so you make an ideal employee. You need work to be intellectually demanding and do not enjoy tedious routines.

In relationships, you anger quickly if faced with stupidity or deception, though you are just as quick to forgive and forget. Emotionally, there are times when your heart rules your head.

Moon in Capricorn

The Moon in Capricorn makes you popular and likely to come into the public eye in some way. The watery Moon is not entirely comfortable in the Earth sign of Capricorn and this may lead to some difficulties in the early years of life. An initial lack of creative ability and indecision must be overcome before the true qualities of patience and perseverance inherent in Capricorn can show through.

You have good administrative ability and are a capable worker, and if you are careful you can accumulate wealth. But you must be cautious and take professional advice in partnerships, as you are open to deception. You may be interested in social or welfare work, which suit your organisational skills and sympathy for others.

Moon in Aquarius

The Moon in Aquarius makes you an active and agreeable person with a friendly, easy-going nature. Sympathetic to the needs of others, you flourish in a laid-back atmosphere. You are broad-minded, fair and open to suggestion, although sometimes you have an unconventional quality which others can find hard to understand.

You are interested in the strange and curious, and in old articles and places. You enjoy trips to these places and gain much from them. Political, scientific and educational work interests you and you might choose a career in science or technology.

Money-wise, you make gains through innovation and concentration and Lunar Aquarians often tackle more than one job at a time. In love you are kind and honest.

Moon in Pisces

You have a kind, sympathetic nature, somewhat retiring at times, but you always take account of others' feelings and help when you can.

Personal relationships may be problematic, but as life goes on you can learn from your experiences and develop a better understanding of yourself and the world around you.

You have a fondness for travel, appreciate beauty and harmony and hate disorder and strife. You may be fond of literature and would make a good writer or speaker yourself. You have a creative imagination and may come across as an incurable romantic. You have strong intuition, maybe bordering on a mediumistic quality, which sets you apart from the mass. You may not be rich in cash terms, but your personal gifts are worth more than gold.

VIRGO IN LOVE

Discover how compatible you are with people from the same and other signs of the zodiac. Five stars equals a match made in heaven!

Virgo meets Virgo

Unlike many same-sign combinations this is not a five-star pairing, for one very good reason. Virgo needs to react with other signs to reveal its hidden best side. Two Virgoans together, although enjoying some happiness, will not present a dynamic, sparkling and carefree appearance. They should run an efficient and financially sound household, but that all-important ingredient, passion, may be distinctly low-key. Star rating: ***

Virgo meets Libra

There have been some rare occasions when this match has found great success, but usually the inward-looking Virgoan depresses the naturally gregarious Libran. Libra appears self-confident but is not so beneath the surface and needs encouragement to develop inner confidence, which may not come from Virgo. Constancy can be a problem for Libra, who also tires easily and may find Virgo dull. A less serious approach from Virgo is needed to make this work. Star rating: **

Virgo meets Scorpio

There are one or two potential difficulties here, but there is also a meeting point from which to overcome them. Virgo is very caring and protective, a trait which Scorpio understands and even emulates. Both signs are consistent, but also sarcastic. Scorpio will impress Virgo with its serious side, and may also uncover a hidden passion in Virgo which all too often lies deep within its Earth-sign nature. Material success is very likely, with Virgo taking the lion's share of domestic chores and family responsibilities. Star rating: ***

Virgo meets Sagittarius

There can be some strange happenings in this relationship. Sagittarius and Virgo view life so differently there are always new discoveries. Virgo is much more of a home bird than Sagittarius, but that won't matter if the Archer introduces its hectic social life gradually. More importantly, Sagittarius understands that it takes Virgo a long time to free its hidden 'inner sprite', but once free it will be fun all the way – until Virgo's thrifty nature takes over. There are great possibilities, but effort is required. Star rating: ***

Virgo meets Capricorn

One of the best possible combinations, because Virgo and Capricorn have an instinctive understanding. Both signs know the value of dedicated hard work and apply it equally in a relationship and other areas of life. Two of the most practical signs, nothing is beyond their ken, even if to outsiders they appear rather sterile or lacking in 'oomph'. What matters most is that the individuals are happy, and with so much in common, the likelihood of mutual material success and a shared devotion to home and family, there isn't much doubt of that. Star rating: *****

Virgo meets Aquarius

Aquarius is a strange sign because no matter how well one knows it, it always manages to surprise, and for this reason, against the odds, it's quite likely that Aquarius will form a successful relationship with Virgo. Aquarius is changeable, unpredictable and often quite 'odd' while Virgo is steady, a fuss-pot and very practical. Herein lies the key. What one sign needs, the other provides and that may be the surest recipe for success imaginable. On-lookers may not know why the couple are happy, but they will recognise that this is the case. Star rating: ****

Virgo meets Pisces

This looks an unpromising match from beginning to end. There are exceptions to every rule, particularly where Pisces is concerned, but these two signs are both so deep it's hard to imagine that they could ever find what makes the other tick. Virgo's ruminations are extremely materialistic, while Pisces exists in a world of deep-felt, poorly expressed emotion. Pisces and Virgo might find they don't talk much, so only in a contemplative, almost monastic, match would they ever get on. Still, in a vast zodiac, anything is possible. Star rating: **

Virgo meets Aries

Neither of these signs really understands the other, and that could easily lead to a clash. Virgo is so pedantic, which will drive Aries up the wall, while Aries always wants to be moving on to the next objective before Virgo is even settled with the last one. It will take time for these two to get to know each other, but this is a great business matching. If a personal relationship is seen in these terms then the prognosis can be quite good, but on the whole, this is not an inspiring match. Star rating: ***

Virgo meets Taurus

This is a difficult basis for a successful relationship, and yet it often works. Both signs are from the Earth element, so have a common-sense approach to life. They have a mutual understanding, and share many interests. Taurus understands and copes well with Virgo's fussy nature, while Virgo revels in the Bull's tidy and artistic qualities. Both sides are committed to achieving lasting material success. There won't be fireworks, and the match may lack a certain 'spiritual' feel, but as that works both ways it may not be a problem. Star rating: *****

Virgo meets Gemini

The fact that both these signs are ruled by the planet Mercury might at first seem good but, unfortunately, Mercury works very differently in these signs. Gemini is untidy, flighty, quick, changeable and easily bored, while Virgo is fastidious, steady and constant. If Virgo is willing to accept some anarchy all can be well, but this not usually the case. Virgoans are deep thinkers and may find Gemini a little superficial. This pair can be compatible intellectually, though even this side isn't without its problems. Star rating: ***

Virgo meets Cancer

This match has little chance of success, for fairly simple reasons: Cancer's generous affection will be submerged by the Virgoan depths, not because Virgo is uncaring but because it expresses itself so differently. As both signs are naturally quiet, things might become a bit boring. They would be mutually supportive, possibly financially successful and have a very tidy house, but they won't share much sparkle, enthusiasm, risk-taking or passion. If this pair were stranded on a desert island, they might live at different ends of it. Star rating: **

Virgo meets Leo

There is a chance for this couple, but it won't be trouble-free. Leo and Virgo view life very differently: Virgo is of a serious nature and struggles to relate to Leo's relentless optimism and cheerfulness and can find it annoying. Leo, meanwhile, may find Virgo stodgy, sometimes dark and uninspiring. The saving grace comes through communication – Leo knows how to make Virgo talk, which is what it needs. If this pair find happiness, though, it may be a case of opposites attract! Star rating: ***

VENUS:
THE PLANET OF LOVE

If you look up at the sky around sunset or sunrise you will often see Venus in close attendance to the Sun. It is arguably one of the most beautiful sights of all and there is little wonder that historically it became associated with the goddess of love. But although Venus does play an important part in the way you view love and in the way others see you romantically, this is only one of the spheres of influence that it enjoys in your overall character.

Venus has a part to play in the more cultured side of your life and has much to do with your appreciation of art, literature, music and general creativity. Even the way you look is responsive to the part of the zodiac that Venus occupied at the start of your life, though this fact is also down to your Sun sign and Ascending sign. If, at the time you were born, Venus occupied one of the more gregarious zodiac signs, you will be more likely to wear your heart on your sleeve, as well as to be more attracted to entertainment, social gatherings and good company. If on the other hand Venus occupied a quiet zodiac sign at the time of your birth, you would tend to be more retiring and less willing to shine in public situations.

It's good to know what part the planet Venus plays in your life for it can have a great bearing on the way you appear to the rest of the world and since we all have to mix with others, you can learn to make the very best of what Venus has to offer you.

One of the great complications in the past has always been trying to establish exactly what zodiac position Venus enjoyed when you were born because the planet is notoriously difficult to track. However, we have solved that problem by creating a table that is exclusive to your Sun sign, which you will find on the following page.

Establishing your Venus sign could not be easier. Just look up the year of your birth on the next page and you will see a sign of the Zodiac. This was the sign that Venus occupied in the period covered by your sign in that year. If Venus occupied more than one sign during the period, this is indicated by the date on which the sign changed, and the name of the new sign. For instance, if you were born in 1950, Venus was in Leo until the 10th September, after which time it was in Virgo. If you were born before 10th September your Venus sign is Leo, if you were born on or after 10th September, your Venus sign is Virgo. Once you have established the position of Venus at the time of your birth, you can then look in the pages which follow to see how this has a bearing on your life as a whole.

1911 VIRGO
1912 VIRGO / 6.9 LIBRA
1913 CANCER / 1.9 LEO
1914 LIBRA / 8.9 SCORPIO
1915 LEO / 29.8 VIRGO /
    21.9 LIBRA
1916 CANCER / 9.9 LEO
1917 LIBRA / 17.9 SCORPIO
1918 LEO / 12.9 VIRGO
1919 VIRGO
1920 VIRGO / 5.9 LIBRA
1921 CANCER / 31.8 LEO
1922 LIBRA / 8.9 SCORPIO
1923 LEO / 28.8 VIRGO /
    20.9 LIBRA
1924 CANCER / 9.9 LEO
1925 LIBRA / 16.9 SCORPIO
1926 LEO / 12.9 VIRGO
1927 VIRGO
1928 VIRGO / 5.9 LIBRA
1929 CANCER / 31.8 LEO
1930 LIBRA / 7.9 SCORPIO
1931 LEO / 28.8 VIRGO /
    20.9 LIBRA
1932 CANCER / 9.9 LEO
1933 LIBRA / 16.9 SCORPIO
1934 LEO / 11.9 VIRGO
1935 VIRGO
1936 VIRGO / 4.9 LIBRA
1937 CANCER / 31.8 LEO
1938 LIBRA / 7.9 SCORPIO
1939 LEO / 27.8 VIRGO /
    19.9 LIBRA
1940 CANCER / 9.9 LEO
1941 LIBRA / 15.9 SCORPIO
1942 LEO / 11.9 VIRGO
1943 VIRGO
1944 VIRGO / 4.9 LIBRA
1945 CANCER / 30.8 LEO
1946 LIBRA / 7.9 SCORPIO
1947 LEO / 27.8 VIRGO /
    .18.9 LIBRA
1948 CANCER / 9.9 LEO
1949 LIBRA / 15.9 SCORPIO
1950 LEO / 10.9 VIRGO
1951 VIRGO
1952 VIRGO / 3.9 LIBRA
1953 CANCER / 30.8 LEO
1954 LIBRA / 7.9 SCORPIO
1955 LEO / 26.8 VIRGO /
    17.9 LIBRA
1956 CANCER / 8.9 LEO
1957 LIBRA / 15.9 SCORPIO
1958 LEO / 10.9 VIRGO

1959 VIRGO / 20.9 LEO
1960 VIRGO / 3.9 LIBRA
1961 CANCER / 30.8 LEO
1962 LIBRA / 8.9 SCORPIO
1963 LEO / 26.8 VIRGO /
    17.9 LIBRA
1964 CANCER / 8.9 LEO
1965 LIBRA / 15.9 SCORPIO
1966 LEO / 9.9 VIRGO
1967 VIRGO / 10.9 LEO
1968 VIRGO / 2.9 LIBRA
1969 CANCER / 29.8 LEO
1970 LIBRA / 8.9 SCORPIO
1971 LEO / 25.8 VIRGO /
    16.9 LIBRA
1972 CANCER / 8.9 LEO
1973 LIBRA / 14.9 SCORPIO
1974 LEO / 8.9 VIRGO
1975 VIRGO / 3.9 LEO
1976 VIRGO / 2.9 LIBRA
1977 CANCER / 29.8 LEO
1978 LIBRA / 8.9 SCORPIO
1979 VIRGO / 16.9 LIBRA
1980 CANCER / 8.9 LEO
1981 LIBRA / 14.9 SCORPIO
1982 LEO / 7.9 VIRGO
1983 VIRGO / 28.8 LEO
1984 VIRGO / 2.9 LIBRA
1985 CANCER / 28.8 LEO
1986 LIBRA / 8.9 SCORPIO
1987 VIRGO / 15.9 LIBRA
1988 CANCER / 7.9 LEO
1989 LIBRA / 13.9 SCORPIO
1990 LEO / 7.9 VIRGO
1991 LEO
1992 VIRGO / 1.9 LIBRA
1993 CANCER / 28.8 LEO
1994 LIBRA / 8.9 SCORPIO
1995 VIRGO / 15.9 LIBRA
1996 CANCER / 7.9 LEO
1997 LIBRA / 12.9 SCORPIO
1998 LEO / 6.9 VIRGO
1999 LEO
2000 VIRGO / 1.9 LIBRA
2001 CANCER / 28.8 LEO
2002 LIBRA / 8.9 SCORPIO
2003 VIRGO / 15.9 LIBRA
2004 CANCER / 6.9 LEO
2005 LIBRA / 10.9 SCORPIO
2006 LEO / 4.9 VIRGO
2007 LEO
2008 VIRGO / 1.9 LIBRA
2009 CANCER / 28.8 LEO

VENUS THROUGH THE ZODIAC SIGNS

Venus in Aries

Amongst other things, the position of Venus in Aries indicates a fondness for travel, music and all creative pursuits. Your nature tends to be affectionate and you would try not to create confusion or difficulty for others if it could be avoided. Many people with this planetary position have a great love of the theatre, and mental stimulation is of the greatest importance. Early romantic attachments are common with Venus in Aries, so it is very important to establish a genuine sense of romantic continuity. Early marriage is not recommended, especially if it is based on sympathy. You may give your heart a little too readily on occasions.

Venus in Taurus

You are capable of very deep feelings and your emotions tend to last for a very long time. This makes you a trusting partner and lover, whose constancy is second to none. In life you are precise and careful and always try to do things the right way. Although this means an ordered life, which you are comfortable with, it can also lead you to be rather too fussy for your own good. Despite your pleasant nature, you are very fixed in your opinions and quite able to speak your mind. Others are attracted to you and historical astrologers always quoted this position of Venus as being very fortunate in terms of marriage. However, if you find yourself involved in a failed relationship, it could take you a long time to trust again.

Venus in Gemini

As with all associations related to Gemini, you tend to be quite versatile, anxious for change and intelligent in your dealings with the world at large. You may gain money from more than one source but you are equally good at spending it. There is an inference here that you are a good communicator, via either the written or the spoken word, and you love to be in the company of interesting people. Always on the look-out for culture, you may also be very fond of music, and love to indulge the curious and cultured side of your nature. In romance you tend to have more than one relationship and could find yourself associated with someone who has previously been a friend or even a distant relative.

Venus in Cancer

You often stay close to home because you are very fond of family and enjoy many of your most treasured moments when you are with those you love. Being naturally sympathetic, you will always do anything you can to support those around you, even people you hardly know at all. This charitable side of your nature is your most noticeable trait and is one of the reasons why others are naturally so fond of you. Being receptive and in some cases even psychic, you can see through to the soul of most of those with whom you come into contact. You may not commence too many romantic attachments but when you do give your heart, it tends to be unconditionally.

Venus in Leo

It must become quickly obvious to almost anyone you meet that you are kind, sympathetic and yet determined enough to stand up for anyone or anything that is truly important to you. Bright and sunny, you warm the world with your natural enthusiasm and would rarely do anything to hurt those around you, or at least not intentionally. In romance you are ardent and sincere, though some may find your style just a little overpowering. Gains come through your contacts with other people and this could be especially true with regard to romance, for love and money often come hand in hand for those who were born with Venus in Leo. People claim to understand you, though you are more complex than you seem.

Venus in Virgo

Your nature could well be fairly quiet no matter what your Sun sign might be, though this fact often manifests itself as an inner peace and would not prevent you from being basically sociable. Some delays and even the odd disappointment in love cannot be ruled out with this planetary position, though it's a fact that you will usually find the happiness you look for in the end. Catapulting yourself into romantic entanglements that you know to be rather ill-advised is not sensible, and it would be better to wait before you committed yourself exclusively to any one person. It is the essence of your nature to serve the world at large and through doing so it is possible that you will attract money at some stage in your life.

Venus in Libra

Venus is very comfortable in Libra and bestows upon those people who have this planetary position a particular sort of kindness that is easy to recognise. This is a very good position for all sorts of friendships and also for romantic attachments that usually bring much joy into your life. Few individuals with Venus in Libra would avoid marriage and since you are capable of great depths of love, it is likely that you will find a contented personal life. You like to mix with people of integrity and intelligence but don't take kindly to scruffy surroundings or work that means getting your hands too dirty. Careful speculation, good business dealings and money through marriage all seem fairly likely.

Venus in Scorpio

You are quite open and tend to spend money quite freely, even on those occasions when you don't have very much. Although your intentions are always good, there are times when you get yourself in to the odd scrape and this can be particularly true when it comes to romance, which you may come to late or from a rather unexpected direction. Certainly you have the power to be happy and to make others contented on the way, but you find the odd stumbling block on your journey through life and it could seem that you have to work harder than those around you. As a result of this, you gain a much deeper understanding of the true value of personal happiness than many people ever do, and are likely to achieve true contentment in the end.

Venus in Sagittarius

You are lighthearted, cheerful and always able to see the funny side of any situation. These facts enhance your popularity, which is especially high with members of the opposite sex. You should never have to look too far to find romantic interest in your life, though it is just possible that you might be too willing to commit yourself before you are certain that the person in question is right for you. Part of the problem here extends to other areas of life too. The fact is that you like variety in everything and so can tire of situations that fail to offer it. All the same, if you choose wisely and learn to understand your restless side, then great happiness can be yours.

Venus in Capricorn

The most notable trait that comes from Venus in this position is that it makes you trustworthy and able to take on all sorts of responsibilities in life. People are instinctively fond of you and love you all the more because you are always ready to help those who are in any form of need. Social and business popularity can be yours and there is a magnetic quality to your nature that is particularly attractive in a romantic sense. Anyone who wants a partner for a lover, a spouse and a good friend too would almost certainly look in your direction. Constancy is the hallmark of your nature and unfaithfulness would go right against the grain. You might sometimes be a little too trusting.

Venus in Aquarius

This location of Venus offers a fondness for travel and a desire to try out something new at every possible opportunity. You are extremely easy to get along with and tend to have many friends from varied backgrounds, classes and inclinations. You like to live a distinct sort of life and gain a great deal from moving about, both in a career sense and with regard to your home. It is not out of the question that you could form a romantic attachment to someone who comes from far away or be attracted to a person of a distinctly artistic and original nature. What you cannot stand is jealousy, for you have friends of both sexes and would want to keep things that way.

Venus in Pisces

The first thing people tend to notice about you is your wonderful, warm smile. Being very charitable by nature you will do anything to help others, even if you don't know them well. Much of your life may be spent sorting out situations for other people, but it is very important to feel that you are living for yourself too. In the main, you remain cheerful, and tend to be quite attractive to members of the opposite sex. Where romantic attachments are concerned, you could be drawn to people who are significantly older or younger than yourself or to someone with a unique career or point of view. It might be best for you to avoid marrying whilst you are still very young.

VIRGO:
2008 DIARY PAGES

October

2008

1 WEDNESDAY ☿ *Moon Age Day 1   Moon Sign Libra*

When it comes to communicating with others you should be very definitely in your element at the present time. There is very little happening that will faze you, even if surprises come thick and fast. A short journey of some sort could prove to be extremely interesting and might also help you to improve your finances.

2 THURSDAY ☿ *Moon Age Day 2   Moon Sign Scorpio*

You seem to be at your best when surrounded by those you love and trust. There is a slight tendency at the moment for you to be rather suspicious about one or two individuals. Although you can sometimes be too pessimistic and negative for your own good, your present tendency to look on the black side might not be misplaced.

3 FRIDAY ☿ *Moon Age Day 3   Moon Sign Scorpio*

Household matters and issues from the past now have a great significance in your life as a whole. As this working week draws to a close you have the chance to catch up on any little jobs that have been left on the shelf for too long. Once things are neat and tidy again, you can afford to be much happier with yourself.

4 SATURDAY ☿ *Moon Age Day 4   Moon Sign Sagittarius*

Now is the time to go for gold in any sporting activity and to register the fact that you can be very competitive at the moment. Not everyone around you will take kindly to losing but this isn't even an option for Virgo at present. Friends you meet socially may have something interesting to impart and you could well be in the mood for having fun.

5 SUNDAY   ☿ *Moon Age Day 5   Moon Sign Sagittarius*

A day to get busy, particularly if there are things to do that have been waiting a while. You need to be very organised, though there is nothing remotely strange about that as far as Virgo is concerned. Keep up appearances when in company and show just how jolly you can be. A little embarrassment is possible today.

6 MONDAY   ☿ *Moon Age Day 6   Moon Sign Sagittarius*

Trends assist you to be very opinionated at the moment, and although that can be good in terms of getting your own way, it probably won't make you quite as popular as you can sometimes be. No matter what happens it would be very sensible to retain a little diplomacy and to use some tact when dealing with important people.

7 TUESDAY   ☿ *Moon Age Day 7   Moon Sign Capricorn*

With the Moon now in your solar fifth house it looks as though you should have very little trouble attracting others socially. Even if the good things in life seem to come along of their own accord, in reality this is down to your careful planning and actions in the past. You can afford to be quite definite when giving instructions today.

8 WEDNESDAY   ☿ *Moon Age Day 8   Moon Sign Capricorn*

You could find finances easier to deal with than of late, particularly if you can get your partner or family members to take your advice in some way. You could also be enjoying a few indulgences under present trends and may be attracted to physical luxury. It's worth making your home welcoming to acquaintances around now.

9 THURSDAY   ☿ *Moon Age Day 9   Moon Sign Aquarius*

You can get well into the thick of things in a work sense, and should have necessary tasks going like clockwork. Part of your real skill at the present time lies in getting others to follow your lead and even to work on your behalf. At your tactful best you can instruct almost anyone – without them realising that it is happening.

10 FRIDAY ☿ *Moon Age Day 10 Moon Sign Aquarius*

This might be a time during which you can show those who know you the best that you are rather more assertive than might sometimes be the case. This is assisted by the planet Mars, which presently occupies your solar third house. The same planetary influence can enhance your ability to speak out for people you see as being exploited.

11 SATURDAY ☿ *Moon Age Day 11 Moon Sign Aquarius*

If you have lots to keep you occupied, it looks as though today could be fast and furious. If anything you will need more time to fit in everything you want to do. Much of what you undertake at the moment might be away from the immediate environs of your home, though tomorrow could present a very different picture.

12 SUNDAY ☿ *Moon Age Day 12 Moon Sign Pisces*

Certain plans could receive something of a setback, and you would be wise to acknowledge the presence of the lunar low, even if you would rather just push on as normal. You might feel a definite urge to indulge yourself in some way, and since other planetary trends focus on family members, your home really counts now.

13 MONDAY ☿ *Moon Age Day 13 Moon Sign Pisces*

Even if things are nowhere near as busy as they were a couple of days ago, you can relish the peace and quiet that is now available to you. For some it will be as if you are resting in the eye of a hurricane because no matter how much is whizzing around you, very little of it may have a bearing on you personally.

14 TUESDAY ☿ *Moon Age Day 14 Moon Sign Aries*

Once again that slightly awkward position of Mars shows itself. This suggests difficulties in communication and a slight tendency for you to be more touchy than usual. Some of your incentives are now a little too ego-based, and a touch more humility would be no bad thing. This is particularly true in any professional setting.

15 WEDNESDAY ☿   *Moon Age Day 15   Moon Sign Aries*

The Sun remains strong in your solar second house. This offers a chance for you to concentrate on firming up securities of one sort or another and to devote much of your energy at present towards making yourself feel more comfortable. A day to be active and enterprising, and to capitalise on chance happenings.

16 THURSDAY ☿   *Moon Age Day 16   Moon Sign Taurus*

Any chance to broaden your horizons should now be grasped with both hands, and you can gradually increase the pace of life throughout today. Learning experiences will also be welcome, and no matter what your age it will be possible for you to make some stunning realisations. The adage 'you're never too old to learn' is especially true now.

17 FRIDAY   *Moon Age Day 17   Moon Sign Taurus*

If there are changes and alterations to take on board, and this might mean having to react quickly to life – possibly in a way that makes you feel a little uncomfortable. Actually it does you no harm at all to be put on the spot, and if nothing else proves to you that you are more than capable of reacting to circumstances.

18 SATURDAY   *Moon Age Day 18   Moon Sign Gemini*

Since some sort of mental peak is available right now, your persuasive talents are highlighted in great measure. You can put these to excellent use when it comes to business or even family matters. Save some time for simple enjoyment, and avoid getting so involved in paradoxes and conundrums that you fail to enjoy yourself.

19 SUNDAY   *Moon Age Day 19   Moon Sign Gemini*

Your mind can work like lightning at the moment, which is fine as long as you don't jump to conclusions that are definitely not founded in reality. Before you make any bold statement or commit yourself to a cause you might eventually regret, it would be sensible to take time out. You would hate to look like a fool later.

20 MONDAY
Moon Age Day 20   Moon Sign Cancer

You can make this an especially productive period as far as your finances are concerned, and you shouldn't have any trouble at all getting others to follow your lead when it comes to monetary matters. Today responds best if you are wise and, typical of Virgo, careful and even frugal in your spending. Friends may be vague.

21 TUESDAY
Moon Age Day 21   Moon Sign Cancer

This is a period during which you have scope to communicate especially well with friends. The whole tenor of your life is changing gradually as the Sun nears its new solar third house position and you can ensure that the direct contact you have with the world at large becomes ever more important in the days and weeks ahead.

22 WEDNESDAY
Moon Age Day 22   Moon Sign Leo

The Moon now in your solar twelfth house assists you to be slightly quieter for a day or two, though not so much that anyone who didn't know you well would recognise. When it comes to learning of any sort it looks as though a period of some enlightenment is on offer – a time when many things could become much clearer.

23 THURSDAY
Moon Age Day 23   Moon Sign Leo

The position of the Sun now overwhelms that of the Moon, and even if you still retreat into yourself at times today, in the main you can be more sociable, and happiest when in the warm glow of affection. This is now as important when it comes from colleagues or acquaintances as when it is evident in the case of your partner.

24 FRIDAY
Moon Age Day 24   Moon Sign Virgo

This is definitely the right time to impress someone with your ideas and know-how. The lunar high assists you to be dominant, very aspiring and good to know. Winning others round should be no problem at all and you should discover that you have what it takes to be a real leader, even if you sometimes don't know where you are going!

25 SATURDAY   *Moon Age Day 25   Moon Sign Virgo*

You should be able to accomplish a lot today, and most of it without undue effort. Whereas you often work very hard to achieve your objectives, you now have what it takes to make others work hard on your behalf. Don't be afraid to be very definite when standing up for the rights of anyone you want to support.

26 SUNDAY   *Moon Age Day 26   Moon Sign Virgo*

For the third day in a row the Moon occupies your own zodiac sign and as a result this may not be a quiet or relaxing sort of Sunday. On the contrary you may be full of beans, as cheerful as can be and anxious to get some fun into your own life, as well as that of your partner. Your romantic side can definitely be put on show now.

27 MONDAY   *Moon Age Day 27   Moon Sign Libra*

Communication will not be helped by a tendency towards arguments today, even if you are not the one who is causing the problems. Such situations only get in the way of the sort of progress you are now in a position to make, which is why you would be wise not to get involved at all. If necessary, spend most of today working on your own.

28 TUESDAY   *Moon Age Day 28   Moon Sign Libra*

All the time the Sun in its present position urges you onto ever-greater social possibilities and emphasises your need to mix with new and interesting people. Your intellectual curiosity is aroused and you relish surroundings that are stimulating and different. There are no fetters placed around the Virgo mind at the moment.

29 WEDNESDAY   *Moon Age Day 0   Moon Sign Scorpio*

Even if unexpected demands are now placed upon you, trends assist you to take the situation very much in your stride. You might have to be a little more patient with people who seem determined to frustrate your efforts, but you do have a great capacity at present to laugh and shrug your shoulders.

30 THURSDAY   *Moon Age Day 1   Moon Sign Scorpio*

Beware of getting involved in needless debates, especially when it is obvious that there is no reasonable solution possible. If people refuse to see your point of view you are just going to have to prove yourself practically. When they see that what you suggest can become a tangible reality, you can persuade them to follow your lead.

31 FRIDAY   *Moon Age Day 2   Moon Sign Sagittarius*

You should now be able to capitalise well on social and communication matters. Make the most of plenty of activity, much of which is inspired by you in the first place. There might not be as much time for work as you would wish but when it comes to enjoying yourself the sky is the limit, both now and across the upcoming weekend.

November

2008

1 SATURDAY — Moon Age Day 3 — Moon Sign Sagittarius

This would be an ideal day to spend time in a family setting, though you may not be sitting around in a chair knitting. On the contrary, you should be filled with energy and doing all you can to spur others into action too. If your spirits are high, woe betide anyone who tries to throw a spanner in the works.

2 SUNDAY — Moon Age Day 4 — Moon Sign Sagittarius

Although today can still be very enjoyable, there could be a slight tendency for you to get carried away with your own big ideas. You can get plenty of help if you need it, and probably also some timely advice. The problem is that Virgo doesn't always listen as much as it might, and difficulties could be the result.

3 MONDAY — Moon Age Day 5 — Moon Sign Capricorn

Rather than putting across your point of view a little forcefully early this week, in all honesty you might get on better if you relaxed more. A day to hang fire with certain projects and ideas, whilst you get existing jobs out of the way. If you don't crowd your schedule you should remain more relaxed and better to know.

4 TUESDAY — Moon Age Day 6 — Moon Sign Capricorn

Communication is well starred today and is made even more harmonious by the fact that the Sun remains strong in your solar third house. What this does for you is to make it easier for you to let people know exactly how you feel about almost anything. Your Virgoan tendency to be locked inside yourself is now absent.

5 WEDNESDAY   *Moon Age Day 7   Moon Sign Aquarius*

Not everyone is going to appreciate it if you speak your mind today, and if there are any difficulties regarding your outspoken manner, these are likely to be at work. In other spheres of your life things are going to be very different, because from a social point of view you can persuade everyone you meet to listen to your opinions.

6 THURSDAY   *Moon Age Day 8   Moon Sign Aquarius*

You have scope to tune in to the emotional state of those with whom you interact today. This will be especially true in the case of your partner or loved ones, but is also somewhat the case in more casual relationships. If you are sensitive, people are more likely to recognise the fact and to single you out for their confessions.

7 FRIDAY   *Moon Age Day 9   Moon Sign Aquarius*

Things could remain somewhat tenuous as far as finances are concerned. It's not that anything is necessarily going wrong, more that you don't recognise the sort of momentum regarding money that makes Virgo happy. In a more personal sense you have what it takes at the moment to bring extra zip into your romantic life.

8 SATURDAY   *Moon Age Day 10   Moon Sign Pisces*

With the lunar low comes what might turn out to be the quietest and least eventful time you will experience during November. If you can't make any headway, then you might as well take a break. You may decide that a few tasks that probably seemed necessary yesterday can now take their place at the back of your mind and are not really urgent at all.

9 SUNDAY   *Moon Age Day 11   Moon Sign Pisces*

Even if some matters are a little off course, you still won't have the energy available to wade into life with your usual appetite. On the contrary, you can afford to leave quite a few things to colleagues and friends, whilst you adopt a sort of dreamy attitude. This is quite natural and even crucial for Virgo from time to time.

10 MONDAY
Moon Age Day 12   Moon Sign Aries

There are signs that you could have your work cut out in personal attachments today, though in the main you can be far more cheerful and reactive than has been the case across the weekend. Any advice you give others will probably come from the reservoir of experience you have accumulated throughout the years.

11 TUESDAY
Moon Age Day 13   Moon Sign Aries

Trends encourage you to let someone you meet today challenge your preconceptions and get you thinking along radical new lines. Be careful though, because important information could go astray at the worst possible time. That's why it is very important to check and double-check all communications today.

12 WEDNESDAY
Moon Age Day 14   Moon Sign Taurus

Generosity is the keyword today, and this means more than throwing a pound or two into the nearest charity tin. On the contrary, you can put yourself out significantly in order to help people you recognise as being in emotional pain or distress. You can even be of help in some ways that you will never realise.

13 THURSDAY
Moon Age Day 15   Moon Sign Taurus

During this time new opinions offer you scope for a radical change in your point of view, and once again this is a trend that comes courtesy of the Sun in your solar third house. It takes a lot for Virgo to change its mind about the fundamentals of life, but that is exactly what you can achieve if you remain broadly open-minded today.

14 FRIDAY
Moon Age Day 16   Moon Sign Gemini

If professional developments seem to be rather hard-going, you might have to rely more on the help and advice of colleagues. This won't go down especially well if you have been in open competition with one or two of them, but despite yourself you could make a new friend as a result of your present needs.

15 SATURDAY
Moon Age Day 17   Moon Sign Gemini

Despite the current focus on mental dexterity, you might recognise within yourself a certain flightiness and unreliability. This won't please you at all because it runs contrary to your mental self-image. But although it won't please you, it could be a source of some small amusement to others and makes you appear all the more human to them.

16 SUNDAY
Moon Age Day 18   Moon Sign Cancer

Right now there is room for some very pleasurable encounters, and this is definitely a Sunday during which you can afford to take time out for personal enjoyment. Who knows what awaits you out there in the big, wide world? It's a case of being present to recognise the possibilities, so be prepared to get out of bed early and take part.

17 MONDAY
Moon Age Day 19   Moon Sign Cancer

Minor disagreements are possible today, even if you are not the one who is actually creating them. More patience will be required in order to deal with such situations and you may also have to do a few jobs more than once because of the incompetence of others. Why not find time for a social gathering in the evening?

18 TUESDAY
Moon Age Day 20   Moon Sign Leo

This is a better day during which to put yourself in the social mainstream, and you can attract a wonderful response from almost anyone you meet. Not that you are leaving anything to chance at the moment. On the contrary, your strength lies in your desire to check and double-check all details.

19 WEDNESDAY
Moon Age Day 21   Moon Sign Leo

It's possible that a personal matter could become common knowledge, particularly if someone can't keep their mouth shut. Your best response is to take this in your stride and don't get annoyed or embarrassed about it. It's worth seeking help and sympathy, even from the most unlikely people.

20 THURSDAY *Moon Age Day 22   Moon Sign Leo*

Don't be afraid to seek out a little solitude today because by tomorrow things could become very busy and you may not have any time to yourself. You need an hour or two to address issues that have been building up for a few days, and things always work out better for you when you can put matters through the mill that is your active mind.

21 FRIDAY *Moon Age Day 23   Moon Sign Virgo*

Personal matters are now positively spotlighted, and it looks as though you can attract a wealth of compliments. Put this together with all the attention you can command, and it becomes obvious that the lunar high is really doing you some favours this month. Finances can be strengthened now.

22 SATURDAY *Moon Age Day 24   Moon Sign Virgo*

This is a time during which it's worth putting more faith in Lady Luck. This doesn't mean putting your shirt on the next horse running, but does insist that you throw in your lot with fortune in less financial ways. A better attitude becomes possible if you are dealing with an old and rather difficult family issue.

23 SUNDAY *Moon Age Day 25   Moon Sign Libra*

New initiatives in the romantic department could allow some Virgo subjects to make this a very interesting and maybe even a fairly surprising sort of Sunday. If you have been looking for a new relationship, this is one of the times of the year to keep your eyes open. First dates should work out well, but established attachments are favoured too.

24 MONDAY *Moon Age Day 26   Moon Sign Libra*

Trends encourage you to make yourself comfortable with the help of loved ones at home. Fix something that is broken, or at least get someone else to do it for you, and don't put up with second-best in anything. Virgo is now at its organisational best and needn't settle for anything less than perfection.

25 TUESDAY *Moon Age Day 27   Moon Sign Scorpio*

Mental competitiveness is stimulated, though some of your efforts could be slightly misplaced unless you check everything out as carefully as you have been doing recently. A gift of some sort is now a possibility, maybe a very late birthday present or a very early Christmas one. You might even decide to treat yourself a little today.

26 WEDNESDAY *Moon Age Day 28   Moon Sign Scorpio*

Most of your real fulfilment is now bound up in home and family, and this tendency is only going to get stronger in the days and weeks ahead. Little Mercury is in your solar fourth house and the Sun has joined it there. Things are lining up very well for December and for the strong family time that Christmas represents to Virgo.

27 THURSDAY *Moon Age Day 29   Moon Sign Scorpio*

Both the luminaries are now in your solar house of home and family, strengthening the focus on your nearest and dearest, as well as on the surroundings that make you feel most comfortable. Demands that come in from outside could suddenly feel less important or even less relevant than they did before.

28 FRIDAY *Moon Age Day 0   Moon Sign Sagittarius*

Romantic affairs are now even more positively highlighted, and the accent is definitely on affairs in the case of some Virgo subjects. Try as best you can to keep your attachments out in the open, because clandestine meetings have potential to leave you feeling both guilty and somehow less honest. Why not find friends in whom you can confide?

29 SATURDAY *Moon Age Day 1   Moon Sign Sagittarius*

You can take advantage of a period of great nostalgia, which is not unusual as the nights become longer and winter really takes hold. It's worth sticking to your favourite people this weekend, though this doesn't mean locking yourself into your own castle. Friends could prove to be just as important to you now as family members.

30 SUNDAY

Moon Age Day 2   Moon Sign Capricorn

An even greater boost to romance is proffered by the Moon today, and you also need to be making the very most of social encounters and happenings. If there is nothing in your diary for this evening, be prepared to arrange something yourself. You can persuade friends to join in, especially if the conversation is stimulating.

December
2008

1 MONDAY
Moon Age Day 3   Moon Sign Capricorn

Private and intimate matters could seem to be far more interesting and rewarding today than public appearances of any sort. Virgo's secretive side is enhanced at the moment, and you might only share your innermost feelings with a very small selection of people. Make sure others don't think you are sulking or scheming.

2 TUESDAY
Moon Age Day 4   Moon Sign Capricorn

With the Moon in its present position you are unlikely to become sidetracked regarding any major hard work. On the contrary, there appears to be no limit to your abilities where concentration and persistence are concerned. If you need assistance you can get it, though Virgo should be very self-reliant at the present time.

3 WEDNESDAY
Moon Age Day 5   Moon Sign Aquarius

You have what it takes to discover someone's true feelings today, and no matter what you have been told in the past there is more to learn right now. In order to get to the bottom of things you might have to delve quite a lot, but you are certain to find the effort worthwhile. It's worth involving friends in social situations.

4 THURSDAY
Moon Age Day 6   Moon Sign Aquarius

You needn't let domestic issues distract you for very long. Sorting things out is what you were born to do, and today should prove to be no exception. Everyone turns to Virgo when level-headed responsibility is required, and in reality the fact that they do should please you.

5 FRIDAY
Moon Age Day 7   Moon Sign Pisces

You would be wise to keep your plans on ice until the lunar low passes and leaves you with a greater chance of success and more energy. Don't be too quick to take on extra responsibilities or to begin sorting out something very complex to do with family members. Your level of patience may not be as high as usual.

6 SATURDAY
Moon Age Day 8   Moon Sign Pisces

Even if you are not succeeding as much as you would wish in the outside world, you can build an interesting and diverting world inside your own head. Your dreamy side is emphasised at the moment, which may not please you all that much. But we all need to visit our own personal fantasy worlds from time to time – even Virgo!

7 SUNDAY
Moon Age Day 9   Moon Sign Pisces

A return to a more 'go-ahead' period is now available – at least it will be after the middle of today. Since this is a Sunday it is possible that the remnants of the lunar low will be slept away as you lie in, but come the afternoon you should once again be moving forward progressively. The time is right to give some thought to a new financial strategy.

8 MONDAY
Moon Age Day 10   Moon Sign Aries

You have scope to take more control over your working life at this time, and need not be in the least fazed if someone tries to give you more responsibility. On the contrary, it is something you are likely to welcome. However, before you take it on maybe you should ask yourself if you are going to be better off as a result.

9 TUESDAY
Moon Age Day 11   Moon Sign Aries

It looks as though you could now be in the market for anything new or unusual. Even if there is something distinctly odd about some of the happenings of today, this is meat and drink to your present nature. Most important of all is your ability to enjoy the company of other people.

10 WEDNESDAY   *Moon Age Day 12   Moon Sign Taurus*

You have what it takes to make family relationships very cordial, and even where there has been a little tension of late you will now be able to establish a lasting truce. Certain people don't annoy you as much as they normally would and this has nothing at all to do with the way they are behaving. The fact is that Virgo can be very tolerant at present.

11 THURSDAY   *Moon Age Day 13   Moon Sign Taurus*

A more competitive, ego-based attitude is to the fore, and Mars in your solar fourth house encourages you to turn to your home with ideas of change and a slightly revolutionary attitude. If some people haven't been pulling their weight recently, this is an ideal time to let them know.

12 FRIDAY   *Moon Age Day 14   Moon Sign Gemini*

You can get practical issues and general run-of-the-mill situations running smoothly, leaving you time to turn towards new projects and different ways of addressing old problems. Friends could be constantly seeking your attention at the moment, especially if they recognise how much they can rely on you.

13 SATURDAY   *Moon Age Day 15   Moon Sign Gemini*

With so much happening in your solar fourth house at the moment there is no wonder that your home environment and the people in it turn out to be the most important aspects of life for you. This would be a good time to confide in relatives, and an especially fortunate period for making a special fuss of your partner.

14 SUNDAY   *Moon Age Day 16   Moon Sign Cancer*

Your desire to please others – which is genuine at present – could fall flat if they refuse to allow you into their world. Don't be too worried about this because in a few days you can get things back to normal. Instead of dwelling on things, why not keep yourself busy and think up a new way to deal with issues that have been troubling you for a while?

15 MONDAY
Moon Age Day 17   Moon Sign Cancer

Your powers of attraction are particularly strong at present and you shouldn't have to work very hard in order to get others on your side. Be prepared to think up some new social strategies and to organise others if they seem ready to accept your advice. If Virgo is working at its best, you should be very content with your lot.

16 TUESDAY
Moon Age Day 18   Moon Sign Leo

It would be a mistake to believe everything you hear today because there may be some people around who will be doing all they can to mislead you. It takes someone very clever to get one over on the average Virgoan, but you might be just a little easier to fool at present. In the main you can afford to remain fairly quiet today.

17 WEDNESDAY
Moon Age Day 19   Moon Sign Leo

Trends continue to support your withdrawal, maybe to the extent that others will think there is something wrong with you. This is less likely in the case of those who know you intimately because they will be used to your occasional sojourns into yourself. This would be a good time to think up a new way forward at work.

18 THURSDAY
Moon Age Day 20   Moon Sign Virgo

All the deep thought of the last couple of days can now be turned to your advantage as the lunar high offers you boundless energy and a very cheerful attitude to life generally. This is a time for fresh starts and for taking a few chances. Your physical condition is also well accented, enabling you to work extremely hard.

19 FRIDAY
Moon Age Day 21   Moon Sign Virgo

A day to get an early start with all important projects and new developments. Fate may be ready to lend a helping hand and you can also make the most of more luck than seems to have been the case recently. Almost everyone you meet will be easy to deal with and will want to offer you the very best of what they can be.

20 SATURDAY   *Moon Age Day 22   Moon Sign Libra*

You should now be able to get the best of all worlds from domestic matters, whilst at the same time continuing to be very practical in the way you approach life. Although you could have an urge to get out and about today, thoughts of Christmas and the final arrangements you have to make could persuade you to stay at home.

21 SUNDAY   *Moon Age Day 23   Moon Sign Libra*

It is at this stage of December that you may well be dragged kicking and screaming into the maelstrom that is the social side of Christmas. Strangely enough, once things get going you can be the life and soul of any party to which you are invited. Virgo is generally a much better social animal than it considers itself to be.

22 MONDAY   *Moon Age Day 24   Moon Sign Scorpio*

Prepare yourself to make a very good impression on almost everyone today. You have scope to achieve that delicate balance between still getting things done and also contributing to the Christmas spirit. At some times today you can even afford to play the fool, particularly if you want to entertain others.

23 TUESDAY   *Moon Age Day 25   Moon Sign Scorpio*

This is a very good day to indulge in information-gathering, and hardly anything happens that is beneath your personal interest. Trends encourage you to listen to gossip much more than you normally would and to respond in kind with chitchat of your own. A day to seek out good friends with whom you share old memories.

24 WEDNESDAY   *Moon Age Day 26   Moon Sign Scorpio*

Don't overestimate the strength of character that you possess – or your ability to put important new plans into action, despite the proximity of Christmas. By this evening you might feel ready for a rest, but the demands of a family life, together with the party atmosphere of Christmas Eve, could ensure you don't get much!

25 THURSDAY   *Moon Age Day 27   Moon Sign Sagittarius*

Christmas Day this year could turn out to be extremely happy for most Virgo subjects. Once again you can show that great balance between getting necessary chores out of the way and also having fun. People will pitch in to lend a hand, and if they don't you can find quite definite ways of prodding them into compliance.

26 FRIDAY   *Moon Age Day 28   Moon Sign Sagittarius*

High spirits prevail, and with planetary influences about that suggest you needn't take yourself at all seriously, you may well shock one or two people with your antics. Personal attachments flourish under present trends, and you have what it takes to find ever better ways to express both your love and your passion.

27 SATURDAY   *Moon Age Day 0   Moon Sign Capricorn*

This is a good time to finally peel off that Virgo veneer and to allow everyone to see what sort of a person you really are. Creative endeavours are favoured, and you might discover that one or two of those presents you received are both thoughtful and fascinating. People might actively seek you out at all stages today.

28 SUNDAY   *Moon Age Day 1   Moon Sign Capricorn*

A strong romantic influence is in evidence, and that should be great as far as your deepest attachments are concerned. However, Mars is in your solar fifth house from today, indicating that inconsequential chatter is less likely to inspire you than it did across the earlier days of Christmas. All the same you can afford to remain generally cheerful.

29 MONDAY   *Moon Age Day 2   Moon Sign Capricorn*

You have scope to show a great appetite for life and to seek out new things to do and alternative ways of getting ahead. Some Virgo subjects could be getting just a little restless if there seems to be nothing to do except eat and drink, though most of you can easily find ways to occupy your intellects, and should be on fine form socially.

30 TUESDAY   *Moon Age Day 3   Moon Sign Aquarius*

Practical, common-sense matters are now to the fore once again.
You need to get on with something useful, even if your actions go
against the grain as far as certain other people are concerned.
Fortunately you should also be quite diplomatic at present and so
can find ways to get round awkward types.

31 WEDNESDAY   *Moon Age Day 4   Moon Sign Aquarius*

It looks as though Virgo is more determined than ever to hog the
social limelight for any New Year party that is on offer. Mercury,
your ruling planet, is now in your solar fifth house. This enhances
your creative side and also acts as a strong stimulant to love and
romance. You may decide to end the year very demonstratively!

VIRGO:
2009 DIARY PAGES

VIRGO:
2009 IN BRIEF

From the moment you begin this year you will be quite aware that extra effort is necessary if you really want to get ahead. January and February offer you the opportunity to be right on top, but only if you sort things out first. Relationships are likely to feel secure and there could be slightly more money coming your way, especially in February.

March and April could prove to be somewhat confusing, and you will have to put in a little extra effort if you really want to get on well at work. All manner of relationships should be working well for you around this time and romantic attachments are especially inclined to look both secure and happy. Look up people from the past, and despite the time of year get out of the house to breathe in as much fresh air as you possibly can.

With the early summer you are likely to be keen to get ahead in many different ways, and the level of energy and enthusiasm during May and June should bring a marked improvement in your fortunes. Not everyone is working on your behalf at this time and you need to watch out for the possibility of being duped in some way. Turn on your intuition and all should be well. You won't achieve perfection at this time but you could come fairly close, and that should be a good incentive to your efforts.

The hottest months of the year, July and August, will really work for you. A number of different planetary influences come together to offer you better co-ordination, good communication skills and a really strong desire to travel. If you are holidaying at this time, be prepared for some really fascinating discoveries, and though you might have to work hard to hold onto money, more should be coming your way. Spend wisely and only after due deliberation.

As the days shorten significantly and autumn begins to show itself you remain pretty much in charge of your life. You won't give up responsibilities you have worked hard to amass and you should also find that family commitments are proving to be more significant than ever. You will still maintain an urge to travel and you certainly will not settle for second-best in business, social matters or love. People who come into your life at this time will probably have a very important part to play in the months and years ahead.

The last two months of the year, November and December, will see you making greater advances still towards some of your chosen objectives. There should be plenty to play for in the career stakes and you remain very much aware that it is your own effort that counts. The Christmas period will find you full of beans and really anxious to make everyone as happy as you should be feeling yourself. Achieving a genuine Christmas spirit will be easy for you

January

(M)

2009

1 THURSDAY
Moon Age Day 5   Moon Sign Aquarius

Today should mark a good start to the year but you do need to get as much done as you can. By tomorrow you might be running out of steam, and this could be a problem so close to the start of the year. For the moment you have what it takes to make a solid impression on life and to persuade colleagues to listen to you.

2 FRIDAY
Moon Age Day 6   Moon Sign Pisces

Today the Moon enters the zodiac sign of Pisces, bringing that part of the month known as the lunar low. Pisces is your opposite zodiac sign, so you may be lacking in energy and not at all sure about the way forward. Your best response is to rely on the assistance you can get from others and avoid making major decisions until Sunday.

3 SATURDAY
Moon Age Day 7   Moon Sign Pisces

A slight lack of confidence typifies this time and you need to be very sure of yourself today before you back any hunch or put forward radical new proposals. On the whole such things are best left until after the weekend. For now you may decide to stay in the bosom of your family, but don't be surprised if you are not at your best.

4 SUNDAY
Moon Age Day 8   Moon Sign Aries

Now much more favourable progress is possible, but whether or not you pick up on the fact on a Sunday remains to be seen. At least certain inexplicable delays can now be dealt with, and you can afford to be fairly sure of your actions. Seeking advice from someone older or wiser than you would be no bad thing.

73

5 MONDAY   *Moon Age Day 9   Moon Sign Aries*

Ego energies rise to the surface at the start of this week as Mars shows itself strongly in your solar fifth house. Now is the time to have fun, and to use your skills to persuade others to join in. Any minor obstacles early in the day can be dealt with quickly and efficiently as you plough on regardless.

6 TUESDAY   *Moon Age Day 10   Moon Sign Taurus*

The urge for freedom is paramount at the moment, encouraging you to fight hard against any sort of restriction. The focus is on personal rights under present planetary trends, and you probably won't be at all enamoured of a 'nanny state' that seems to constantly tread on your toes. Virgo can be very outspoken, and also well informed.

7 WEDNESDAY   *Moon Age Day 11   Moon Sign Taurus*

This is an excellent time to put yourself in the limelight. The Sun is in your solar fifth house, supporting your efforts to attract attention. This is certainly not always the case for Virgo because you do have a tendency to retreat into yourself on occasions. For the moment, your gregarious and sociable side is definitely highlighted.

8 THURSDAY   *Moon Age Day 12   Moon Sign Gemini*

Be prepared to give material issues and work goals some extra support at this stage of the week. Speaking of goals, this is an ideal time to pursue sporting activities. For once you can be a team player, no matter what you happen to be doing. Getting on well with colleagues and superiors should be a natural aspect of life now.

9 FRIDAY   *Moon Age Day 13   Moon Sign Gemini*

All matters to do with relationships can be strengthened thanks to the present position of Mars in your chart. All shades of variety should appeal to you at the moment, and you needn't sit on the sidelines, even if you don't really understand the rules of the game. What matters the most at this time is getting involved at whatever level.

10 SATURDAY   *Moon Age Day 14   Moon Sign Cancer*

Your spirits remain generally strong, and you have scope to find more and more ways in which to show your creativity. This can be something as simple as making minor changes in and around your home, but it could also extend to you taking up new hobbies or pastimes that offer you much more self-expression than usual.

11 SUNDAY   *Moon Age Day 15   Moon Sign Cancer*

An ideal day for working in group environments and for getting yourself out of the house and into new situations. The great outdoors may well appeal to you, even though winter winds may be blowing strongly. It is important at the moment that you can see wide horizons, both inside and outside your mind.

12 MONDAY   ☿   *Moon Age Day 16   Moon Sign Leo*

Trends suggest that a relationship or an intimate issue may require attention, so beware of getting so wrapped up in outside issues that you forget about those close to you. People may have to remind you of your obligations, which is indeed rare in the life of the average Virgo subject. It's just so easy to get sidetracked right now.

13 TUESDAY   ☿   *Moon Age Day 17   Moon Sign Leo*

It may be important now for you to set limits regarding how far you will go to help others. Of course if the person concerned is your partner or a family member you can do that bit more, but there is a danger you will spend so much time working for those in your vicinity that you fail to attend to important matters in your own life.

14 WEDNESDAY ☿   *Moon Age Day 18   Moon Sign Virgo*

Today the Moon enters your own zodiac sign of Virgo, bringing that part of the month known as the lunar high. Energy levels will be enhanced, and you have what it takes to become more certain of yourself. You needn't be afraid to take the odd risk, particularly if you make the most of your level of general good luck.

15 THURSDAY ☿ *Moon Age Day 19   Moon Sign Virgo*

Another fortunate period is on offer, and it could pay to try out your luck today. You can easily get ahead of the game now by being in the right place to score significant points. This could be especially noticeable at work, though there are still occasions when it's worth saying to yourself, 'more haste and less speed'.

16 FRIDAY ☿ *Moon Age Day 20   Moon Sign Libra*

Work in progress has potential to be especially rewarding now, and you can afford to remain generally confident in your own thoughts and actions. The same may not be true with regard to colleagues or friends, and some rather strange behaviour could be the result. A few pointed questions may be the best way forward now.

17 SATURDAY ☿ *Moon Age Day 21   Moon Sign Libra*

You have scope to make this a very pleasant time of the month, and to impress those around you. Bear in mind that if you catch the attention of those in authority, you could be well on the way to gaining their support. All in all you seem to have what it takes to get ahead and to make the best impression on just about anyone.

18 SUNDAY ☿ *Moon Age Day 22   Moon Sign Libra*

What counts for a great deal at the moment is exchanging ideas and 'fact-finding'. Just about anything can enable you to activate your grey cells, allowing you to show time and again just how bright you can be. Be prepared to turn to the written word, in whatever form, to help you to express yourself more fully.

19 MONDAY ☿ *Moon Age Day 23   Moon Sign Scorpio*

Freedom of expression is highlighted right now, and you may not take at all kindly to being restricted in your opinions. What you believe to be true is held deeply in your heart, and it's worth fighting tenaciously to put across your opinions, even when to do so might go against your best interests. All the same, try not to be too stubborn!

20 TUESDAY   ☿   *Moon Age Day 24   Moon Sign Scorpio*

Your strength lies in your talent for dealing with people, and you can really show this at the moment. Your fascination with others is emphasised, and it shouldn't be hard under present trends for you to find out what makes those around you tick. This is also a fine time to express your emotions in terms of love.

21 WEDNESDAY   ☿ *Moon Age Day 25   Moon Sign Sagittarius*

All of a sudden the time is right for you to express yourself through your family and home environment. This is because the Moon is in your solar fourth house, from where it urges you to get to know what really makes others tick. A better understanding all round should be the result, offering you a sense of satisfaction.

22 THURSDAY   ☿ *Moon Age Day 26   Moon Sign Sagittarius*

Right now the focus is on doing things that will utilise your general helpfulness and that let you be as charitable as your nature allows. By all means go to great lengths to prove your love and show your loyalty. It's worth making sure that you aren't putting all that effort into a relationship that is past its sell-by date.

23 FRIDAY   ☿ *Moon Age Day 27   Moon Sign Sagittarius*

With the current position of Venus in your solar chart, the spotlight is on looking good and presenting yourself positively to the world at large. Rather than taking only a moment or two to prepare yourself in the morning, there is much to be said for spending more time than usual looking in the mirror and getting things right.

24 SATURDAY   ☿ *Moon Age Day 28   Moon Sign Capricorn*

You may well insist on being number one today, which is great as far as you are concerned but can be quite tiresome to others. Trends encourage you to build your own self-confidence, possibly at the expense of others. A little more thought would be no bad thing when it comes to your general approaches today.

25 SUNDAY ☿ *Moon Age Day 29   Moon Sign Capricorn*

Ego fulfilment is increasingly emphasised. It isn't enough to suspect that you are loved – you want to be told. Eliciting the response you want from others might not be very easy, especially if they are busy or otherwise engaged. Instead of standing outside and trying to attract their attention, why not pitch in and help?

26 MONDAY ☿ *Moon Age Day 0   Moon Sign Aquarius*

Be prepared to do everything you can to ensure that things are going well in your working environment. This means knowing not only what is expected of you but also how other people are having a bearing on situations. The time is right to listen to colleagues and to do what you can to make their lot easier, as well as your own.

27 TUESDAY ☿ *Moon Age Day 1   Moon Sign Aquarius*

The successful touch you have with the world at large is much emphasised today. You have what it takes to make progress as a result of things you did in the dim and distant past, and as usual in your life you can prove that nothing is wasted. Charming others and turning heads count for a great deal under present influences.

28 WEDNESDAY ☿ *Moon Age Day 2   Moon Sign Aquarius*

There are signs that routines will suit you much more than they do some of the people with whom you live and work. You like to know what is expected of you, and it should be no problem for you to do things time and again in the same way. Variety is the spice of life, but in the case of Virgo constancy is often more important.

29 THURSDAY ☿ *Moon Age Day 3   Moon Sign Pisces*

A day to stay cool, calm and collected because the lunar low is around, and rushing or pushing too much won't guarantee the best results. Rather than expecting to get too much done, your best approach is to work through any particular task to its logical conclusion. Good luck may be hard to find just now.

30 FRIDAY ☿ *Moon Age Day 4   Moon Sign Pisces*

The natural securities and the smooth running of your life could be thrown into turmoil today unless you guard what you have very carefully. This is not the best time of the month to spend lavishly or to take chances with relationships. You can get everything back to normal tomorrow, though things could still look odd at present.

31 SATURDAY ☿ *Moon Age Day 5   Moon Sign Aries*

If you allow your real abilities to surface again, you can bring back order after the potential chaos of the last couple of days. Don't be too quick to leap into situations you don't understand, for the first part of the weekend you would be wise to stick to what is familiar. Family relationships are to the fore.

February 2009

1 SUNDAY
Moon Age Day 6   Moon Sign Aries

It's worth being sensitive to the impression you get from others.
Your best approach is to listen carefully to what people have to say,
and not to push your luck or to go where you know you might feel
insecure. This is the least positive side of Virgo at work, but in the
main you can get most things going your way.

2 MONDAY
Moon Age Day 7   Moon Sign Taurus

Social and travel matters have potential to keep you very busy this
week, and you can start things as you mean them to go on – hectic!
New starts are possible at work, perhaps with a reorganisation of
some kind. If you make the most of what today offers, you should
be far happier with your lot than you expected.

3 TUESDAY
Moon Age Day 8   Moon Sign Taurus

Trends now assist you to achieve short-term goals, and you may not
be looking too far ahead as far as your work is concerned. However,
this is an ideal time to lay down plans for journeys you want to make
later in the year, and to get together with family members in order
to discuss something important.

4 WEDNESDAY
Moon Age Day 9   Moon Sign Taurus

There are good reasons to put yourself in the limelight today,
especially with your employer or someone who is potentially
important to your future. The spotlight is on education and
training, and there are gains to be made for Virgo in these areas,
even if not everyone you come across is easy to deal with.

5 THURSDAY   *Moon Age Day 10   Moon Sign Gemini*

Even if you have more than enough energy to get through any task that faces you today, a part of your nature might simply want to spend the day chatting and listening to what others have to say. You can afford to be extremely sociable at this time, and can learn a great deal by making sure you are in the mainstream of opinions.

6 FRIDAY   *Moon Age Day 11   Moon Sign Gemini*

Close and even intimate involvement with others is the area of life upon which you are encouraged to focus right now. Romance is available for many Virgo subjects, and you can make this evening extremely interesting in terms of a promise that is being made. Friends might be expecting much of you, but they shouldn't be disappointed.

7 SATURDAY   *Moon Age Day 12   Moon Sign Cancer*

Mercury offers a personal boost to your life and a time when you can make sure you are in tune with the world at large. By all means take a casual approach to compliments you attract, though in reality you can use them to boost your confidence. In situations that demand definite skills, you can now be a winner.

8 SUNDAY   *Moon Age Day 13   Moon Sign Cancer*

Material considerations could well be less important to you today than inner satisfaction. Of course it's always good to have money, but it's worth realising that no amount of cash can compensate for a happy life. Because of this you might be thinking in terms of a reorganisation that will give you more social time.

9 MONDAY   *Moon Age Day 14   Moon Sign Leo*

Your Virgoan search for perfection and your love of detail can both be used to your advantage during the coming week. If you use your talents well to organise events, you can also feed the strong social impulses that are at the very heart of your nature. This is not a time to fuss about things that are of no real importance.

10 TUESDAY
Moon Age Day 15   Moon Sign Leo

Now is the time to build things up positively in your life. Although the lunar high does not arrive until tomorrow, you should already be thinking about new ways to break the bounds of the possible. The adventurous side of the Virgo nature is rarely as emphasised as it is at the moment, so maybe the fireworks are about to start!

11 WEDNESDAY
Moon Age Day 16   Moon Sign Virgo

Look out, Virgo, because today has potential to be fast and furious. The lunar high is an extremely potent visitor this month, and it urges you to get as much change into your life as proves to be possible. An ideal day to capitalise on the fact that Lady Luck is on your side by trying to fulfil a wish that has been around for ages.

12 THURSDAY
Moon Age Day 17   Moon Sign Virgo

This is the time to take your chances and to be as different as you want to be. Whilst there is always going to be a part of your mind that advises you not to do anything embarrassing, in the main you can now afford to be franker, freer and even sillier than you would ever normally be. People will probably love you for it.

13 FRIDAY
Moon Age Day 18   Moon Sign Libra

It's Friday the thirteenth today, but you needn't allow your superstitious side to get in the way of your continued push. Life generally favours your best efforts, particularly if you can get others to do what they can to help you along. A day to throw your sometimes pessimistic nature out of the window and see life in positive terms.

14 SATURDAY
Moon Age Day 19   Moon Sign Libra

Today responds best if you assert yourself more creatively, whether through artistic pursuits or playing to the gallery. The dramatic side of your nature is highlighted, allowing you to respond in a positive way to the attention you can attract. If you feel as though you don't know yourself – so much the better!

15 SUNDAY
Moon Age Day 20   Moon Sign Scorpio

Your strength now lies in the energy that you can pour into practical and career projects. Of course the work side of this trend might not be appropriate on a Sunday, but that shouldn't stop you finding something concrete to do. The level of interest in your life at the moment is helping you to move on to better and better prospects.

16 MONDAY
Moon Age Day 21   Moon Sign Scorpio

Bringing out the best in others is the keyword this week, and this is a positive trend because it helps you to gain their help and support. It's worth finding time to talk to people at a deeper level and to find out what really makes them tick. Don't be afraid to think about romance and let the light of love shine in your eyes.

17 TUESDAY
Moon Age Day 22   Moon Sign Scorpio

Trends suggest you may now see more significance in your home life than you do in the practical side of life beyond your own front door. This is thanks to the present position of the Moon in your solar fourth house, and it offers you the chance to get closer to family members, particularly those who have a definite need of you.

18 WEDNESDAY *Moon Age Day 23   Moon Sign Sagittarius*

Today you are surrounded by influences that can help you with practical organisation, which is always pleasing to the average Virgo subject. You can get things done in a flash, and should also be able to get others to follow your lead. This helps you to achieve a high degree of personal satisfaction, and perhaps a better financial position.

19 THURSDAY *Moon Age Day 24   Moon Sign Sagittarius*

Your personal drive towards excellence is emphasised, and you needn't take second-best, from either yourself or anyone else. This could make you rather exacting and difficult to cope with. A day for new social possibilities – in fact anything that will prevent you from becoming bogged down with the practical side of life.

83

20 FRIDAY
Moon Age Day 25   Moon Sign Capricorn

Stresses are possible today, caused by a conflict between the demands of work and the need for leisure. Balancing time commitments may be difficult, but it is necessary. If you want to keep all aspects of your life in harmony, you will probably have to work especially hard – though of course you could always call on others for assistance.

21 SATURDAY
Moon Age Day 26   Moon Sign Capricorn

Working with close associates could prove to be very satisfying today, whether at work or around your home. Getting family members to come up trumps is within your capabilities, and you can also make this a very romantic weekend. A day to build a happy atmosphere around you and wallow in the satisfaction this brings.

22 SUNDAY
Moon Age Day 27   Moon Sign Capricorn

You now have what it takes to put your thoughts into words to an even better extent than is usually the case for communicative Virgo. It's time to show your sociability rather than the darker side of your nature, which some could find threatening or intimidating. You have scope to remain powerful but also extremely approachable.

23 MONDAY
Moon Age Day 28   Moon Sign Aquarius

Work situations have potential to be positive if you make the effort to get along with others and remain communicative and interesting to have around. This may prove to be one of the best romantic interludes of the month, and if you whisper words of love at the moment you should be so convincing that nobody could ever doubt you.

24 TUESDAY
Moon Age Day 29   Moon Sign Aquarius

Charm is your forte now, whether amongst casual acquaintances or lovers. In the end it's really all about getting your own way, but if you do this in a charming manner you can convince others that it is you who are handing out the favours. Beware of jumping to irrational conclusions, particularly as far as work-related matters are concerned.

25 WEDNESDAY   *Moon Age Day 0   Moon Sign Pisces*

Any good fortune that you have been harnessing in your life across the last few days might now seem to weaken, though this is a very temporary matter and is down to the arrival of the lunar low. Be prepared to keep up your spirits, and rather than giving in to any irrational doubts, simply prove them to be nonsensical.

26 THURSDAY   *Moon Age Day 1   Moon Sign Pisces*

Trends suggest that responsibilities may be emotionally burdensome at this time, and that some tension is a possibility in your daily life. Your best response is to remember that none of this will seem to be of the least importance by tomorrow, and even by this evening you should be able to get things working positively again.

27 FRIDAY   *Moon Age Day 2   Moon Sign Aries*

You have what it takes to get things back to normal today, with the help of some strong planetary placements in your solar chart that are supporting your efforts to a great extent. Even if you decide that sacrifices have to be made in emotional relationships, the effort should be worthwhile if it makes others happy.

28 SATURDAY   *Moon Age Day 3   Moon Sign Aries*

You may well find that intimate relationships suit you the best today and that casual attachments are less significant. Where money is concerned, trends assist you to make progress, particularly if you can gain the support of your partner. It's worth making sure family members understand fully what you are saying to them.

March

2009

1 SUNDAY
Moon Age Day 4   Moon Sign Aries

Communication could prove to be especially interesting on the first day of March. It may also occur to you that the worst of the winter is likely to be out of the way soon, and that allows you to come out of your shell in a physical sense. Rather than just abandoning some of your clothes, why not let some inhibitions go too?

2 MONDAY
Moon Age Day 5   Moon Sign Taurus

Cultural matters are now favoured as you expand your capacity for communication and your ability to mix with strangers. As a result you can make your social life more and more interesting, and might be discovering things about your own talents that you never realised before. Routines could seem a bit of a chore today.

3 TUESDAY
Moon Age Day 6   Moon Sign Taurus

In a work sense it is important to keep your impatience under wraps because it won't help in the diplomatic stakes. Even if there are people around who don't seem to know what they are supposed to be doing, criticising them isn't the best way forward. Be prepared to offer timely advice and practical help – then everyone wins in the end.

4 WEDNESDAY
Moon Age Day 7   Moon Sign Gemini

Extra charisma helps you to enrich your social life now. You can use your sense of happiness and confidence in your future to give personal relationships a boost, and the present position of the Sun in your solar seventh house supports positive progress. Accolades are a distinct possibility if you prove your level of commitment.

5 THURSDAY
Moon Age Day 8   Moon Sign Gemini

Today offers you scope to make use of your clear-minded approach to life and also your practical common sense. These are qualities that will be so well marked at present that you have little reason to put a foot wrong. In social matters you can afford be more casual and perhaps to follow the lead of someone else.

6 FRIDAY
Moon Age Day 9   Moon Sign Cancer

When it comes to work, trends highlight your enthusiasm and dynamism. Who could fail to notice that you are around right now? Hardly anyone – though there are always going to be certain individuals who don't care for you. There may be very little you can do about this, and probably no reason to worry about it in the first place.

7 SATURDAY
Moon Age Day 10   Moon Sign Cancer

In a social sense you can now benefit from conversations and from listening to what others have to say. Their ideas, when put together with your own, can prove to be extremely useful. A positive attitude towards jobs that need doing around the home can make them go with a swing, though you might still need to get others involved.

8 SUNDAY
Moon Age Day 11   Moon Sign Leo

It might somehow feel as if you are more susceptible to colds and chills right now. That doesn't mean you have to stay in front of the fire. On the contrary, it's worth getting out there in the open, to stare out to sea or climb some peak. The more you cosset yourself, the more likely it is that you will fall foul of some germ or other.

9 MONDAY
Moon Age Day 12   Moon Sign Leo

Even if you are enjoying the company of others a great deal today, you can still find quiet moments. The Moon is in your solar twelfth house, encouraging a more thoughtful interlude when you may favour your own company at some stages of the day. As a result this could be a very mixed bag of a day.

10 TUESDAY   *Moon Age Day 13   Moon Sign Virgo*

You can now make the most of an energy surplus and a strong desire to tackle everything at once. Normally the advice would be to slow down, but whilst the lunar high is around you can afford to crowd your schedule. Better luck is there for the taking, and you have what it takes to get colleagues and friends to gather round you.

11 WEDNESDAY   *Moon Age Day 14   Moon Sign Virgo*

Physical vitality is still the keynote of the day, and you have scope to gear your efforts towards creative activities. This would be a particularly good day for discussions with others, given your ability to remain sensible while keeping your aspirations high. If you don't actually make money today, you can at least plan how to do so.

12 THURSDAY   *Moon Age Day 15   Moon Sign Libra*

Now comes a time to seek out new friends and ways of entertaining yourself that you haven't tried before. The Sun is still in your seventh house, encouraging an interest in anything that is very different from your normal daily routines. You can best curb restlessness by not sitting around thinking about things too much.

13 FRIDAY   *Moon Age Day 16   Moon Sign Libra*

You now have an opportunity to strengthen your financial position, or at least to think of ways of improving your fortunes in the not too distant future. Virgo can be very ingenious, and you certainly needn't let yourself be stuck in ways of doing things that haven't been productive so far. Why not listen to the ideas of friends?

14 SATURDAY   *Moon Age Day 17   Moon Sign Libra*

Your strength now lies in your motivation when it comes to work and your ability to be discriminating at this stage of the month. Even if others fall for glib lines and get-rich-quick schemes, you are far too clever. Not only should you fight shy of being conned yourself, you also have scope to steer others clear of obvious pitfalls.

15 SUNDAY   *Moon Age Day 18   Moon Sign Scorpio*

With your ruling planet, Mercury, prominently placed in your solar chart, your sense of wonder and your natural inquisitiveness are highlighted. A great deal of useful information could be on offer around now, and in order to make the best of it you have to be paying attention. Not everything might work out as you expect today.

16 MONDAY   *Moon Age Day 19   Moon Sign Scorpio*

Even if on the one hand you are now very committed to your work and to practical matters, you may also have a great desire to spend more time with family members. For this you can thank the present position of the Moon. Compromises may well be needed, so be prepared to involve your loved ones in your latest schemes.

17 TUESDAY   *Moon Age Day 20   Moon Sign Sagittarius*

Today's trends indicate a level of impatience, and if you really want to get on well you would be wise to settle down and allow certain matters to mature naturally. There is also much to be said for letting other people do what they understand best, instead of constantly interfering and getting in the way.

18 WEDNESDAY   *Moon Age Day 21   Moon Sign Sagittarius*

Relationships are well starred at present, so any that are not quite working out may need looking at in a different light. It could be that you don't actually dislike a certain person – more that you don't understand them. Your best approach is to make an extra effort to get to know anyone who has caused you problems. The effort is worthwhile.

19 THURSDAY   *Moon Age Day 22   Moon Sign Capricorn*

All pursuits relating to creativity are favoured today. If this isn't the best day of the month when it comes to making a profit, you have to ask yourself whether money is more important than being happy and content with your lot. What you do have scope to gain today is personal satisfaction, which can be worth more than gold.

20 FRIDAY   *Moon Age Day 23   Moon Sign Capricorn*

The time is right to seek support from those around you, either at work or at home. It's also worth looking for new ways to spend leisure hours, and someone you know well might have just the right idea. An ideal day to plan journeys with friends – perhaps even trips that could take place this very weekend.

21 SATURDAY   *Moon Age Day 24   Moon Sign Capricorn*

When it comes to applying yourself practically, it may be difficult to cut the mustard this weekend. For this reason alone you might decide instead to have some fun and to allow some jobs to wait. If you do insist on being in harness today, you will probably only have to plough the same ground again later. Relax – the spring is here!

22 SUNDAY   *Moon Age Day 25   Moon Sign Aquarius*

The focus is on communication with others today, and your efforts should be more than worthwhile. It's worth taking a little journey if you can and meeting people you don't see very often. Other types of communication can also put you in the know, but there is nothing like face-to-face contact right now.

23 MONDAY   *Moon Age Day 26   Moon Sign Aquarius*

Some situations have to be grubbed up at the root before you can plant something new, and that might well be the case at present. You need to recognise that there are things you will have to get rid of before you can move on. A spring-clean would be no bad thing, though this may involve more than sorting through your sock drawer.

24 TUESDAY   *Moon Age Day 27   Moon Sign Pisces*

Minor tensions are possible today with the Moon in your opposite zodiac sign. Try to avoid allowing these to get in your way, and don't over-react to the smallest difficulties. It might be best to spend some time on your own, because it would be very hard to fall out with yourself. Routines could offer some comfort now.

25 WEDNESDAY   *Moon Age Day 28   Moon Sign Pisces*

The influence of the lunar low might leave you wondering whether you'll be able to get things to work out the way you wish, or whether you'll have to modify some of your plans. Think all you want, but beware of taking any precipitous action, because in a day or two things could look different. You are Mr or Miss Pessimistic today!

26 THURSDAY   *Moon Age Day 0   Moon Sign Pisces*

You can best avoid disagreements with others today by showing your willingness to listen. Present planetary trends highlight your strong will, and you might not always admit that you can be wrong. A day to keep in touch with relatives and make sure you don't forget something that is of great importance to a loved one.

27 FRIDAY   *Moon Age Day 1   Moon Sign Aries*

Among all the other planetary activity, the Sun has moved into your solar eighth house. For the next four weeks or so this supports a more decisive Virgo who is willing to change almost anything to achieve some long-term improvements. Prepare to make the most of a time of significant reorganisation and progress.

28 SATURDAY   *Moon Age Day 2   Moon Sign Aries*

Along with the Sun, little Mercury has also passed from your seventh to your eighth house, and this may be even more significant. It isn't what you say that matters at the moment but the way you say it. Even if you are rather offhand on occasions, there is no doubting that your perception is good and that your words carry strength.

29 SUNDAY   *Moon Age Day 3   Moon Sign Taurus*

Trends indicate a more competitive Virgo with a keener sense of purpose. This should be a good thing in most circumstances, but it might also get you into a little trouble if you don't temper your attitude with a degree of diplomacy. In the heat of a discussion it is hard to count to ten before you respond – but it's definitely worth a try.

30 MONDAY
Moon Age Day 4   Moon Sign Taurus

Intense thinking is the key, and you can use your strong intuition to get to the root of any problem and to sort it out almost immediately. Things that you usually deal with in a couple of minutes may take much longer, particularly if you are very exacting. Not an ideal day for trying to fly high in the money stakes.

31 TUESDAY
Moon Age Day 5   Moon Sign Gemini

You are now in the middle of a potentially hard-working period, and there may not be too much time for enjoyment – or at least that's the way it might look from your side of the fence. You may also have to deal with the demands of friends. The best way forward today is to make compromises and to leave some work until later.

April

2009

1 WEDNESDAY

Moon Age Day 6   Moon Sign Gemini

Once again there is an overemphasis on your need to be assertive, which isn't helped in the least by a seventh-house Mars. Personal relationships could be prone to disruptions during this period, and you would be wise to tread carefully in order to avoid upsetting certain people. Despite this, progress is possible at work.

2 THURSDAY

Moon Age Day 7   Moon Sign Cancer

A faster pace of events is indicated, as is the need to get about more. Those Virgo subjects who have chosen this time to take a break or a journey could be the luckiest of all because variety is what you need, even if you don't realise the fact. It won't be long before you can put certain worries to rest once and for all.

3 FRIDAY

Moon Age Day 8   Moon Sign Cancer

An ideal day to consider whether you can continue with a personal matter, or even a relationship of some sort, in the same old way. It's worth looking at things in a fresh light, and the best way to do that is from a distance. Beware of being too assertive or over-anxious about details in disputes. Try not to get in a fluster today.

4 SATURDAY

Moon Age Day 9   Moon Sign Leo

A slight withdrawal from the social world may seem necessary now that the Moon is in your solar twelfth house, but it would at least allow you to feel more content and less anxious. A quieter social scene this weekend may suit you better, but if you do have to be in company, you should still be able to manage.

5 SUNDAY
Moon Age Day 10   Moon Sign Leo

You can now make gains, either emotionally or financially, by being astute and willing to look at an alternative point of view. You also have scope to improve your domestic life by restructuring things to make your surroundings more comfortable. Be prepared to welcome people from the past back into your life.

6 MONDAY
Moon Age Day 11   Moon Sign Virgo

This would be a really good time to consolidate recent gains and also to show just how capable you are. The lunar high offers an opportunity to capitalise on good luck and to put just the right amount of effort into anything you undertake. As a result, you can make sure this is a fascinating and useful sort of day.

7 TUESDAY
Moon Age Day 12   Moon Sign Virgo

This is a time of potential good fortune when you can make progress, almost without having to try too hard. Make the most of promising invitations, and of the fact that the effort you have put in recently should now be starting to pay significant dividends. Your ability to increase your popularity knows no bounds now.

8 WEDNESDAY
Moon Age Day 13   Moon Sign Virgo

You can still get things going your way, at least during the first part of the day. By the time the afternoon comes along there could be one or two little complications to deal with, but nothing that should get in your way for very long. In the main you are able to put a definite full stop to tasks that have been around for quite some time.

9 THURSDAY
Moon Age Day 14   Moon Sign Libra

Getting into heated debates with anyone today could prove counter-productive. Rather than arguing about something that may not be very important in any case, your best approach is simply to bite your tongue. If you do allow yourself to get involved in matters that are not really within your province, you may well regret it later.

10 FRIDAY
Moon Age Day 15   Moon Sign Libra

Don't miss out on any important news that is doing the rounds today. Your argumentative side is less emphasised, assisting you to find out how others really feel and to learn what they know. By keeping your ear to the ground today you could get ahead in a project that will enable you to make significant progress in your life.

11 SATURDAY
Moon Age Day 16   Moon Sign Scorpio

If you keep your mind steady and focused, you are more likely to achieve a great deal more than if you are excitable and changeable in your opinions. Even amazing situations need to be dealt with in that famous Virgoan way at the moment. Meanwhile, the Sun in your solar eighth house is still urging change.

12 SUNDAY
Moon Age Day 17   Moon Sign Scorpio

Little Mercury comes up trumps for you again today. Mercury is your ruling planet, and is ideally placed for you today when it comes to getting your message across to an often unsuspecting world. Now is the time to surprise others by coming up with an idea that should suit everyone. Don't let today drag – do something amazing!

13 MONDAY
Moon Age Day 18   Moon Sign Sagittarius

Recent events, which may have been running at a fantastic pace, can be slowed down significantly for the next couple of days. This is not to suggest that you need to let life become dull or uninteresting. However, you can afford to think more about home and family, and to concentrate more across the board.

14 TUESDAY
Moon Age Day 19   Moon Sign Sagittarius

Getting along with everyone you meet is unlikely to be the easiest thing in the world, particularly if there are individuals around now who annoy you simply by being alive. All Virgo people have their likes and dislikes, but your best response at the moment is to stay patient and don't react – even if provoked.

15 WEDNESDAY *Moon Age Day 20   Moon Sign Sagittarius*

The more leisure and pleasure you can get into your life at this stage of the week, the better you should feel about things generally. Rather than allowing yourself to get bogged down with pointless jobs, the time is right to enhance your own importance and self-confidence. Routines are probably for the birds at the moment.

16 THURSDAY *Moon Age Day 21   Moon Sign Capricorn*

The spotlight is now on new horizons and unconventional approaches to life. Short journeys may well suit you, together with anything that gets your grey cells going. There are gains to be made by pitting yourself against some sort of competition, and making sure there is enough going on to make you feel really alive.

17 FRIDAY *Moon Age Day 22   Moon Sign Capricorn*

Much of the effort you put into today affords a degree of progress that should please you no end. Even if others help, the real fact is that you have what it takes to contribute to just about everything going. Although there's a danger of tiring yourself out by your efforts, you can at least go to bed feeling generally content.

18 SATURDAY *Moon Age Day 23   Moon Sign Aquarius*

Relationships are so much emphasised today that it's worth going to great lengths to strengthen them and to make sure you feel content with your lot. Romance is possible, perhaps when you least expect it, and trends assist you to be really on the ball when it comes to finding special words of love that can make all the difference.

19 SUNDAY *Moon Age Day 24   Moon Sign Aquarius*

Venus in your solar seventh house helps you to promote a state of harmony in your life generally. Eliciting help from loved ones can assist you to get things done with half the usual effort. This is a Sunday that is ideal for spending in the bosom of your family, or at the very least with people you have known for quite some time.

20 MONDAY   *Moon Age Day 25   Moon Sign Aquarius*

You continue to have what it takes to get on well, even if there are individuals around who seem less capable, and who may well call upon your ability to sort things out. This shouldn't bother you at all, particularly if you manage to come up with the right answers for them. After all, it's nice to feel needed!

21 TUESDAY   *Moon Age Day 26   Moon Sign Pisces*

As today gets underway, your spirits could well be lower than they have been for the last few days. This is because the lunar low is around, bringing a period when it might feel as though you are climbing a sizeable mountain, especially at work. Even if you remain in good spirits socially, you might still choose to spend some time alone.

22 WEDNESDAY   *Moon Age Day 27   Moon Sign Pisces*

Beware of expecting miracles from plans and objectives today. Be prepared to settle for second-best, or better still, avoid doing more than you have to. Not everyone around you might be equally helpful today, and you may even have problems with those closest to you. You have scope to make tomorrow a better day.

23 THURSDAY   *Moon Age Day 28   Moon Sign Aries*

You have what it takes to avoid getting as hung up on material things as might sometimes be the case. Your strength lies in seeing through to the heart of life and realising that it is personal contentment that really matters. Almost everything else is some sort of illusion, and enlightened Virgo should now be able to see this.

24 FRIDAY   *Moon Age Day 29   Moon Sign Aries*

One-to-one relationships might need some special attention today. Even if you are not promoting family arguments, you could find that you are involved in any case. The best way to avoid confrontation today is to back down, and that is something that Virgo is often reluctant to contemplate.

25 SATURDAY   *Moon Age Day 0   Moon Sign Taurus*

This is an excellent period for taking the initiative when it comes to changes you want to make around yourself, especially in your home circumstances. You have what it takes to get other people to lend a hand, especially those who are on the same wavelength as you are. Look out for opportunities to meet other Virgo subjects.

26 SUNDAY   *Moon Age Day 1   Moon Sign Taurus*

Increased social activity is possible, and you can allow your intellectual curiosity to be aroused at every turn. Rather than sitting around doing nothing, there is much to be said for getting some fresh air today. Why not blow away the cobwebs with a trip out? Even if it's raining, you can wear a coat! Fun can be found with friends.

27 MONDAY   *Moon Age Day 2   Moon Sign Gemini*

Emotional pressure in partnerships is enhanced by Mars in your solar eighth house. If you feel you aren't working at your best in social settings, ask yourself whether there are awkward people around who seem determined to get on the wrong side of you. What you have to deal with may simply be a clash of personalities.

28 TUESDAY   *Moon Age Day 3   Moon Sign Gemini*

The Sun is now in your solar ninth house, supporting a need to expand your personal horizons as much as proves to be possible. This is therefore a period when travel is favoured, and if you have arranged a fairly early holiday of some sort, so much the better. Even very short journeys of discovery are well starred now.

29 WEDNESDAY   *Moon Age Day 4   Moon Sign Cancer*

This would be another good day to take a trip or to plan something very different and exotic. A less positive option would be to follow the same old routines all day long. Be prepared to identify something you can look forward to, whilst at the same time discovering new ways to get your mind working. Romance is highlighted today.

30 THURSDAY   *Moon Age Day 5   Moon Sign Cancer*

An ideal time to develop your negotiating skills at work and to prove just how good you are as a diplomat. You have scope to capitalise on a potential winning streak when it comes to finances, and to reap the rewards from plans you laid down some time ago. A day to keep looking and thinking ahead.

May

2009

1 FRIDAY
Moon Age Day 6   Moon Sign Cancer

The first day of May is a time for keeping major objectives in your mind, whilst at the same time finding some place in the day for having fun. In some situations it's worth watching and waiting, and although this can be quite frustrating it is nevertheless valuable. If you are suspicious about someone today, leave them alone!

2 SATURDAY
Moon Age Day 7   Moon Sign Leo

The present position of the Sun constantly allows you to see new prospects and ways to broaden your personal horizons. At the same time there is a quieter aspect to today because the Moon is occupying your solar twelfth house. Slow and steady wins the race at work, even if you feel as though your mind and body are not in accord.

3 SUNDAY
Moon Age Day 8   Moon Sign Leo

You can take advantage of another slightly quieter day and a period during which you would be wise to think more than act. You can afford to allow others to take the strain somewhat, whilst you catch up on plans for the immediate future. The dreamy side of Virgo is emphasised today, and there may be little you can do to get away from it.

4 MONDAY
Moon Age Day 9   Moon Sign Virgo

Progress should be within your grasp this morning, and today represents a potentially ideal start to a new week. With the lunar high in attendance, you shouldn't put a foot wrong, and you have what it takes to work towards greater personal accolades. You can also persuade colleagues and friends to help out if required.

5 TUESDAY   *Moon Age Day 10   Moon Sign Virgo*

Financial good fortune could be there for the taking at this time, and your efforts to get ahead are assisted by both this and the co-operation you can elicit from those around you. There is much to be said for remaining progressive in your thinking and for putting your efforts and your talents into exciting new projects.

6 WEDNESDAY   *Moon Age Day 11   Moon Sign Libra*

It is important today to emphasise what you believe to be true, even if other people have different ideas. This could cause difficulties for you, though that shouldn't matter in the long run. Your integrity is one of your most important possessions and you are famous for it. It's worth asking friends to support your plans.

7 THURSDAY   ☿   *Moon Age Day 12   Moon Sign Libra*

This is a dramatic period for the expansion of your horizons. The Sun is in your solar ninth house, and that is especially supportive of journeys, and particularly travel to exotic locations. Anything that gets you thinking in a new and slightly revolutionary way is grist to the mill now, and happiness could well follow.

8 FRIDAY   ☿   *Moon Age Day 13   Moon Sign Scorpio*

Plenty of different interests may seem more stimulating today than concentrating in any one particular direction. This is not unusual for Virgo because you have the sort of mind that is always looking in new directions. What will bring the most satisfaction today is seeing that ideas you have been developing for a while are paying off.

9 SATURDAY   ☿   *Moon Age Day 14   Moon Sign Scorpio*

You need to move as swiftly as possible today, because present planetary trends don't encourage letting the grass grow under your feet. Success can be achieved by being in the right place to make things happen, and this is as important in your social life as it will be at work. Romance is to the fore around now.

10 SUNDAY ☿ *Moon Age Day 15   Moon Sign Scorpio*

Trends encourage you to think more about home and family today, and with the Moon in your solar fourth house you may decide that this is the best time of all for confronting any domestic issue that has been waiting for a while. Discussions with those around you can bring positive times to come, and much can be achieved.

11 MONDAY ☿ *Moon Age Day 16   Moon Sign Sagittarius*

You can now use your excellent insight to work out how others are likely to react under any given circumstance. This can be very useful, and it even allows you to manipulate situations to a great extent. If your partner has been behaving somewhat oddly of late, now is an ideal time to find out exactly why.

12 TUESDAY ☿ *Moon Age Day 17   Moon Sign Sagittarius*

Optimism and a sense of adventure are the legacies of a ninth-house Sun, and this same planetary position also assists you to charm others. If there are colleagues or associates who don't seem to have been too keen on you before, now is the time to get them on your side. Be prepared to use your winning ways.

13 WEDNESDAY ☿ *Moon Age Day 18   Moon Sign Capricorn*

Today responds well if you keep on the move and refuse to entertain thoughts of resting. All the same, you do have scope to make time for a little luxury in your life, and to use any spare moments to make a special fuss of your partner. Most important of all at present is your ability to be witty and funny.

14 THURSDAY ☿ *Moon Age Day 19   Moon Sign Capricorn*

When it comes to getting down to brass tacks, the world shouldn't find you wanting at this time. Mars remains in your solar eighth house, offering an edge to your nature that others will recognise instinctively. A day to make sure that your way of doing things becomes the norm, and that your strategy or technique is what counts.

15 FRIDAY   ☿ *Moon Age Day 20   Moon Sign Capricorn*

Beware of expecting everything to go your way today. It isn't that you suddenly lack incentive or know-how, it's just that with the Moon in its present position you may not be quite as decisive as you have been. Definite bloomers can be best avoided by relying on the good offices of colleagues or friends, and by accepting advice.

16 SATURDAY   ☿ *Moon Age Day 21   Moon Sign Aquarius*

In personal attachments you can now afford to be more intuitive and shouldn't have any trouble working out why those you love are behaving in the way they are. You can use this to stay one step ahead of them and to do things that will please them no end. Make the most of the high degree of natural kindness that is evident now.

17 SUNDAY   ☿ *Moon Age Day 22   Moon Sign Aquarius*

Your present strong intuition is emphasised even more today, and is a commodity that can help you no end. This is a great period for sharing your deepest feelings and emotions, and your insights into the way those around you are likely to react can be quite remarkable. This is Virgo at its best, so make sure everyone takes notice!

18 MONDAY   ☿   *Moon Age Day 23   Moon Sign Pisces*

Frustration is a distinct possibility today, and with the lunar low around your best approach is to move carefully in your association with the world at large. It doesn't matter how cautious you are, there might still be pitfalls you didn't see in advance. The trend only lasts a day or two, and with extra attention you can remain confident.

19 TUESDAY   ☿   *Moon Age Day 24   Moon Sign Pisces*

Trends discourage you from getting carried away with your own big ideas today. Although under normal circumstances these tend to be very useful and effective, little problems could arise at the moment. If you seek help and support from people who are definitely in the know, you have a chance to mitigate any real difficulty.

20 WEDNESDAY ☿   *Moon Age Day 25   Moon Sign Aries*

New material interests are there for the taking, and many of them have genuine value and profit. With the lunar low now completely out of the way you have more chance of progress and of capitalising on general good fortune. A day to avoid being stuck in one place for any longer than is strictly necessary.

21 THURSDAY ☿   *Moon Age Day 26   Moon Sign Aries*

Make the most of any opportunities to increase your overall influence, especially in work situations. In a more social sense you can now afford to take a slightly less dominant role, and perhaps also to try something new that demands a level of learning on your part. A slightly less assertive Virgo is a legacy of today's trends.

22 FRIDAY   ☿   *Moon Age Day 27   Moon Sign Aries*

It's time to explore the wider world beyond your door, and planetary trends now support travel and adventure. This would be an excellent period in which to take a holiday or even any short trip that stimulates your mind and exercises your body. Getting in tune with your environment should be part of your response to today.

23 SATURDAY ☿   *Moon Age Day 28   Moon Sign Taurus*

Mars remains fixed in your solar eighth house, urging you to transform your life in one way or another. This can be quite unsettling, because on one level Virgo is a definite creature of habit. Nevertheless, it doesn't do you any harm at all to be shocked out of your routines, and what you replace them with could be amazing!

24 SUNDAY   ☿   *Moon Age Day 0   Moon Sign Taurus*

Mercury in your solar ninth house urges you to be more of a 'seeker', especially when it comes to new ideas and philosophies. The spotlight is on your desire to keep up with what is topical and up-to-date, and this too is part of the legacy of Mercury in its present position. As far as talking is concerned, few people could better you today.

25 MONDAY ☿ *Moon Age Day 1 Moon Sign Gemini*

Where business and practical matters are concerned you have scope to get life going very much your way at the start of this week. Under present planetary trends your strength lies in getting different things to come together, assisted by the advice you can elicit from others. Being in the right place should also help.

26 TUESDAY ☿ *Moon Age Day 2 Moon Sign Gemini*

A calm and rational approach now works best, particularly if loved ones seem to be putting you under a degree of pressure. What you can't afford is to get involved in family arguments. It might be all too easy to be drawn into rows that have nothing to do with you in the first place, but you can always refuse to take part.

27 WEDNESDAY ☿ *Moon Age Day 3 Moon Sign Cancer*

The desire for new mind-broadening experiences remains especially strong at the moment, and there is the possibility of boredom setting in unless you allow yourself a degree of personal freedom. You can still get things done eventually, even if you don't tackle everything today. A day to be with people you find stimulating.

28 THURSDAY ☿ *Moon Age Day 4 Moon Sign Cancer*

Your judgement could be slightly impaired as the Moon moves into your solar twelfth house, so it's worth thinking about things carefully and in a detached manner. Stepping back and looking at your own life may not be easy, but is something that Virgo can generally manage to do. If you're seeking fun, friends could help.

29 FRIDAY ☿ *Moon Age Day 5 Moon Sign Leo*

A little more emotional self-discipline is the key to getting on as well as you would wish today. On a strictly practical level, it would be too easy today to invest funds into situations that look rather odd from the start. Your best approach is to keep your purse or wallet tightly closed, until at least Sunday, after which bargains are more likely.

30 SATURDAY   ☿   *Moon Age Day 6   Moon Sign Leo*

There is one more day to go before the lunar high returns, and you can take advantage of this slightly quieter sort of Saturday – at least until later in the day. By this evening you can get yourself right back on form, and might be quite anxious to get out of the house and have fun. It's time to seek out some very congenial company.

31 SUNDAY   ☿   *Moon Age Day 7   Moon Sign Virgo*

The lunar high comes along and encourages a much more devil-may-care sort of attitude for most Virgo subjects. You can now afford to capitalise on the feeling that you could tackle almost anything by being far more adventurous than of late. Prepare to make the most of romantic opportunities, and to keep your popularity high.

June

2009

1 MONDAY
Moon Age Day 8   Moon Sign Virgo

You have scope to achieve an excellent start to a new working week because just about everything you need to succeed is in place. Trends assist your rise to prominence and your ability to show others that you are both capable and charismatic. Use your skills to the full when it comes to lending a timely hand to a friend.

2 TUESDAY
Moon Age Day 9   Moon Sign Libra

On a practical level you would now be wise to get as much done as you can. Handling half a dozen different jobs at the same time is child's play to you at the best of times, but right now should present no problems at all. A day to persuade others to favour your ideas, and to pursue discussions about new possibilities.

3 WEDNESDAY
Moon Age Day 10   Moon Sign Libra

This would be a first rate time for going somewhere new or for seeing something that really stimulates your mind. From an intellectual point of view you can presently be as bright as a button, and shouldn't easily be fooled by anyone. At work you have a chance to show that you are far more capable than some of the people around you.

4 THURSDAY
Moon Age Day 11   Moon Sign Scorpio

Any sort of contact at a professional level is favoured, though you may have slightly more difficulty in personal situations and attachments. The week is growing older, and if there is something you have been meaning to get done ever since Monday, now is the time to get on with it. Why not enlist some support for social incentives?

5 FRIDAY   *Moon Age Day 12   Moon Sign Scorpio*

It's time for a spring-clean. Venus is now strong in your solar eighth house, and this encourages a readiness to throw out any unwanted or obsolete items that are cluttering up your house. At the same time you can take advantage of this trend to look at old concepts and ideas. Virgo can afford to be quite revolutionary for once.

6 SATURDAY   *Moon Age Day 13   Moon Sign Scorpio*

There is much to be said for seeking excitement, adventure and a real challenge this weekend, but you won't find them by sitting in a chair and waiting. All the incentives are yours to take, and you are also in a position to get others to fall in line with whatever takes your fancy. Love can be strengthened no end today.

7 SUNDAY   *Moon Age Day 14   Moon Sign Sagittarius*

Once again the Moon returns to your solar fourth house, heralding a period of extreme nostalgia. This may be intensified if you are also getting rid of possessions you no longer need. Remember that you are a Virgo subject and that you have a great need for routine. It's one thing being disciplined, but quite another to be ruthless.

8 MONDAY   *Moon Age Day 15   Moon Sign Sagittarius*

You can afford to put a lot of force behind what you think and what you say today. It's worth being slightly careful that you don't offer any unintended offence. If you handle things well, few people should argue with your point of view, and in the main you have scope to get your own way. Younger relatives could be the exception.

9 TUESDAY   *Moon Age Day 16   Moon Sign Capricorn*

Make the most of the news you can gather today, particularly if it is positive. Mental pursuits of one sort or another are just the thing to make you feel as though you are alive and competing, whilst at the same time change and diversity might also appeal. This has potential to be a very busy period, so be ready to reap some rewards.

10 WEDNESDAY   *Moon Age Day 17   Moon Sign Capricorn*

With the Moon in your solar fifth house you have plenty of opportunity to be yourself today. Your strength lies in your ability to get along with other people and to keep those around you smiling virtually all the time. Leisure and romance are highlighted today and for the rest of the week.

11 THURSDAY   *Moon Age Day 18   Moon Sign Capricorn*

Life might now take on a fairly so-so feel, particularly if you are trying to get things organised. If you aren't inclined to push yourself when you are in or around your home, you may decide to save your efforts for when you are out and about. Why not take a trip? Even the change of air could work wonders.

12 FRIDAY   *Moon Age Day 19   Moon Sign Aquarius*

The more opinionated side of your nature is now emphasised, thanks to the present position of Mars in your solar chart. The trouble is that you might be in no mood for any sort of compromise either, and this can be a formidable combination. Diplomacy is your best approach, though that may not be easy at the moment.

13 SATURDAY   *Moon Age Day 20   Moon Sign Aquarius*

Why not try a total change of scenery today if you have the chance to do so? Restlessness tends to prevail at the moment, doing little to assist you with any type of discussion. Even if you simply aren't on sparkling form for much of today, you can certainly help yourself by not sticking around and vegetating.

14 SUNDAY   *Moon Age Day 21   Moon Sign Pisces*

The lunar low has now arrived, and this won't encourage you to speed things up as far as your general life is concerned. This could turn out to be the sort of Sunday that drags – unless of course you take matters into your own hands. Once again you can afford to give in to that almost subconscious urge to do something adventurous!

15 MONDAY   *Moon Age Day 22   Moon Sign Pisces*

If you feel oversensitive today, remember the lunar low. If other people seem difficult to deal with, ask yourself whether at least part of the problem is coming from your direction. A day for getting on with simple tasks and allowing others to do some of the necessary work for you. Be prepared to sit and think at some stage.

16 TUESDAY   *Moon Age Day 23   Moon Sign Pisces*

Although today might seem to start slowly, you can soon speed things up and feel more like your old self. This would be an ideal time to approach friends, particularly if you need to broach a subject you have been avoiding of late. You have what it takes to come up with some good ideas today, and need to try and exploit them.

17 WEDNESDAY   *Moon Age Day 24   Moon Sign Aries*

Communications in the career world are ever more important around now, and the more you express your ideas, the better is the response you can attract. Your confidence should remain generally high, and with a planetary peak on the way you are about to enter one of the best periods for some time. Make the most of it.

18 THURSDAY   *Moon Age Day 25   Moon Sign Aries*

There are signs that you have lots to say for yourself, and for that you can thank the positions of both Mercury and Mars. You can best avoid being too outspoken by tempering your natural tendency to speak your mind with a clear understanding of the way your words will impact on the thoughts and actions of those around you.

19 FRIDAY   *Moon Age Day 26   Moon Sign Taurus*

It looks as though you can afford a more freewheeling attitude, and this might have as much to do with the advancing summer as it does with any particular planetary influence. If the weather is fair, why not take this opportunity to break routines and feel the warm winds on your face? Sticking to one place isn't ideal for today.

20 SATURDAY   *Moon Age Day 27   Moon Sign Taurus*

You can get the most from life today by being flexible in your attitude and by avoiding disputes, especially with family members. Love counts for a great deal this weekend – though it's up to you whether you decide to make the most of it. Creature comforts are not particularly highlighted at this time.

21 SUNDAY   *Moon Age Day 28   Moon Sign Gemini*

Chances are that you can gain most stimulation through mental challenges today, and it's worth creating or finding these for yourself. A good day for doing what you can to ring the changes and for spending time with loved ones. If you're also in the market for a real bargain, there is much to be said for a shopping spree!

22 MONDAY   *Moon Age Day 29   Moon Sign Gemini*

Meetings offer scope for rewards at the start of this week, though it has to be said that you may not be in the mood for too much work. Trends suggest that there are so many other fascinating possibilities about, all of which probably look far more interesting than boring old routines. Socially, it's off with the old and on with the new.

23 TUESDAY   *Moon Age Day 0   Moon Sign Cancer*

Now is the time to draw inspiration from new contacts, and to clearly identify what you want most from life. If you manage to be definite in your approach to others, you should leave them in no doubt as to your thinking or intentions, and you can gain assistance if you need it. Love may prove more interesting today.

24 WEDNESDAY   *Moon Age Day 1   Moon Sign Cancer*

Setting great store by your own notions is fine, but that doesn't mean you can afford to ignore what others are saying. If you at least pay lip service to their opinions you should avoid offering any offence and can make your own path smoother in the long run. Beware of getting involved in problems you already know to be insoluble.

25 THURSDAY
Moon Age Day 2   Moon Sign Leo

Mishaps are possible as part of your everyday routines at the moment, and it's worth being especially careful before you involve yourself in anything you know to be difficult or awkward. Your best approach is to save such tasks for later, and only get cracking on those jobs that are routine, or in which you have the most confidence.

26 FRIDAY
Moon Age Day 3   Moon Sign Leo

By widening your intellectual horizons today you can open new doors that lead into areas of life you haven't looked at before. What you need most at the moment is interest, and even if the Moon in your solar twelfth house takes the edge off things for much of today, by the evening you can capitalise on a more positive influence.

27 SATURDAY
Moon Age Day 4   Moon Sign Virgo

The lunar high arrives and immediately allows you to sweep away some of the cobwebs that have been around for the last few days. The time is right to be adventurous, and the weekend will offer all sorts of possibilities if you are willing to take advantage of them. Be prepared to capitalise on intriguing offers from friends.

28 SUNDAY
Moon Age Day 5   Moon Sign Virgo

If unusual new ventures still appeal to you, you can now get your mind working overtime and dream up a few for yourself. Rather than sticking around at home and getting into domestic routines, you need to be out there showing the world what Virgo is made of. The lunar high should enhance your joyful attitude.

29 MONDAY
Moon Age Day 6   Moon Sign Libra

This is a great time to be with others and probably the best time of the year so far for taking a holiday. The larger the group in which you get involved the better, and Virgo is definitely in a good position to share almost anything. Despite your usual cautious approach to money, spending a little would be no bad thing now.

30 TUESDAY

Moon Age Day 7   Moon Sign Libra

This is not a time to be backward about coming forward, and you have scope to make life your own through your joyful attitude and your willingness to be involved. Your popularity is emphasised, and you can capitalise on this by climbing higher in your chosen career. The opportunity for you to shine has seldom been better.

July
2009

1 WEDNESDAY
Moon Age Day 8   Moon Sign Libra

All of a sudden the focus moves away from excitement and new experiences and onto the search for intellectual companionship and meaningful conversation. The first day of July offers a chance to get in touch with your deeper self and to make the most of the influence of those who can help you open your mind to a different view of life.

2 THURSDAY
Moon Age Day 9   Moon Sign Scorpio

A favourable day for spending more time with your friends. Rather than simply holding to what you know, why not open up to what others are saying. You have scope to make progress in any sort of co-operative venture, because Virgo is in a mood to share. Your usual tendency to hold things to yourself is less apparent now.

3 FRIDAY
Moon Age Day 10   Moon Sign Scorpio

Keep your eyes and ears open for new information that can be used to your advantage. Make the most of the loving attention that you can elicit, and be prepared to seek advice from good friends. Your home life could be the only area that is slightly problematical. Younger people especially might cause you a little anxiety.

4 SATURDAY
Moon Age Day 11   Moon Sign Sagittarius

Mars is still in your solar ninth house, supporting a headstrong attitude at times. This might be most relevant in the event of someone challenging your point of view or refusing to take your advice. As a result you could become slightly prickly and less inclined to co-operate. You may even take your ball and go home!

5 SUNDAY   *Moon Age Day 12   Moon Sign Sagittarius*

Spending time with a close friend or a relative and confiding in them might seem quite inviting on one level today. However, there is a more adventurous side to your nature and you could be torn between two or more options. Since you can't do everything, you need to make a definite decision or split your day somehow.

6 MONDAY   *Moon Age Day 13   Moon Sign Sagittarius*

With energy levels at a peak today there should be no holding you back. Positive influences surrounding you today include ones that are associated with your personal life. Romance is therefore extremely well starred, and you should also be able to enhance your general popularity at the moment.

7 TUESDAY   *Moon Age Day 14   Moon Sign Capricorn*

You now have scope to achieve greater success than ever when it comes to winning over social contacts. New friends can be the result, as well as the chance to mix with the sort of individuals who stimulate your intellect to a greater extent. You have what it takes to overcome any obstacles today, and to enjoy a fairly smooth ride.

8 WEDNESDAY   *Moon Age Day 15   Moon Sign Capricorn*

Once again advancement is possibly as a result of improving your social connections. You needn't give in today if the going gets tougher because that is just the time to put in your maximum effort. All sorts of people can be persuaded to help your progress today, even if it's for reasons of their own.

9 THURSDAY   *Moon Age Day 16   Moon Sign Aquarius*

It does seem as if you have your work cut out today, but that is because of the short-lived position of the Moon. Whilst certain practical issues need thinking through quite carefully, success is still possible if you put in that extra bit of effort. Since rewards might not be easy to achieve, if they do appear they can surprise you.

10 FRIDAY   *Moon Age Day 17   Moon Sign Aquarius*

Contact with friends should be especially favourable today, and therein lay the seeds of your own progress. It is the ideas of those around you that you can use to assist your own success, so it's worth trying to get on well with all manner of people. Later in the day there is room for a return to a more romantic interlude.

11 SATURDAY   *Moon Age Day 18   Moon Sign Aquarius*

Be prepared to stand by your decisions today, and don't allow yourself to be diverted from any path you have chosen. Even if people are trying to talk you round, your intuition is strong, and if it tells you to take a particular course you need to listen carefully. Today can be good socially, and should offer new opportunities.

12 SUNDAY   *Moon Age Day 19   Moon Sign Pisces*

There are lessons to be learned at the moment, and some of these come along thanks to the lunar low. As a result it may not always appear at first that life is going your way, but you do have what it takes to ensure that your efforts are not wasted. Routine responses might have to be modified if you are dealing with family members.

13 MONDAY   *Moon Age Day 20   Moon Sign Pisces*

Fortune might appear to be at an all-time low today, particularly if you are looking on the black side more than of late. Although this may not be the most positive start to any week you have encountered this month, you can still forge your own path – albeit slowly. By tomorrow you can make sure that almost everything looks different.

14 TUESDAY   *Moon Age Day 21   Moon Sign Aries*

You can now benefit your own life through the people you meet in your everyday life. Try to make the most of all social opportunities, and don't be left in the shadows when a chance comes to show what you are worth. It might take time for you to get back up to speed, but by this evening you should be firing on all cylinders again.

15 WEDNESDAY   *Moon Age Day 22   Moon Sign Aries*

Time spent with your lover has potential to be both rewarding and enjoyable today. Trends also encourage a change of scene, so if it is possible to take a day off, this is an ideal time to do it. The more you stimulate your mind, the greater are the opportunities for advancement. There are still strong romantic possibilities around.

16 THURSDAY   *Moon Age Day 23   Moon Sign Taurus*

There is much to be said for an expansion of your field of mental interests around now, and for allowing almost anything to stimulate your imagination. By all means show a positive and forward-looking attitude, though it's worth registering how your own ideas impact on others. Sporting activities are well accented at present.

17 FRIDAY   *Moon Age Day 24   Moon Sign Taurus*

Conflict is now possible between your personal ambitions and what you feel to be your obligations, and it may be difficult to fit in everything you know you should accomplish. Your best response is to think long and hard and then to do only those things you know will not create waves. It may not be easy, but you can win out.

18 SATURDAY   *Moon Age Day 25   Moon Sign Taurus*

Where major ambitions are concerned efficiency is the key, and it wouldn't be sensible to be wasteful today. Your interests are best served by avoiding spending money or expending effort that isn't necessary, and by doing only what is essential to achieve your objectives. It's a lean, mean face to Virgo that turns out to be your ally.

19 SUNDAY   *Moon Age Day 26   Moon Sign Gemini*

Socially speaking this period has potential to be very encouraging. There are good reasons for getting to know new people and forming deeper alliances with those who were only acquaintances before. Finding common ground with the world at large should now be much easier, and you can make firm friends of even unlikely types.

20 MONDAY   *Moon Age Day 27   Moon Sign Gemini*

Once again it is the social side of life that is emphasised the most. For this reason you may not feel much like working hard, even if you know this is the path to success. On the contrary, today offers you scope to let others take the strain, whilst you sit back for a while and supervise. Be prepared to move closer and closer to a dream.

21 TUESDAY   *Moon Age Day 28   Moon Sign Cancer*

You need diplomacy and co-operation today if you are going to reach longed-for objectives, but fortunately you can also put in that famous Virgoan effort again. If you decide to pool your resources with colleagues and friends there is no end to what you can achieve, and sharing should be not only useful now but also enjoyable.

22 WEDNESDAY   *Moon Age Day 0   Moon Sign Cancer*

For much of the time today you can afford to coast along merrily, enjoying the fact that all sorts of situations are sorting themselves out for once. Virgo is used to having to struggle, though it has to be said that for much of the time this is really just a state of mind. If you really feel yourself to be successful – then you will be!

23 THURSDAY   *Moon Age Day 1   Moon Sign Leo*

This is not the best time of the month for getting things to go your way, though this is a very temporary state of affairs and is brought about by the present position of the Moon in your solar twelfth house. This offers a quieter interlude when you may be much less inclined to get involved in anything you see as unsavoury or grubby.

24 FRIDAY   *Moon Age Day 2   Moon Sign Leo*

Once again you would be wise to keep your expectations modest and to plan ahead. By tomorrow the lunar high can offer you a real boost, but for the moment you need to clear the decks for action. It's worth remembering that harsh words, although unpleasant and potentially worrying, are probably a flash in the pan.

25 SATURDAY *Moon Age Day 3   Moon Sign Virgo*

With the lunar high supporting greater self-confidence and that famous Virgo determination, there isn't much that lies beyond your capabilities. You are also now entering a period during which the focus is on travel and seeing new sights. As a result, it's worth thinking about a holiday or at least getting away from routines.

26 SUNDAY *Moon Age Day 4   Moon Sign Virgo*

Much of the short-term future lies in today's decisions, and you need to be aware that a great deal of what you have been hoping for relies on your actions around this time. There is no reason to be nervous about this, particularly if you get Lady Luck on your side and make use of some of the positive ideas that are available.

27 MONDAY *Moon Age Day 5   Moon Sign Libra*

Various ups and downs are possible this week, and some of them could start today. Even if it is necessary to think on your feet more than you have been doing recently, that shouldn't bother you because it allows you to increase the level of excitement on your path through life. Newer and better professional possibilities are on offer.

28 TUESDAY *Moon Age Day 6   Moon Sign Libra*

Professionally speaking you remain bold and ambitious, just the right state of mind to prosper from all chance encounters and new incentives. What shows the most today is that you are quite willing to back your hunches and although you might come unstuck on occasions, in the main what you estimate to be likely will indeed happen.

29 WEDNESDAY *Moon Age Day 7   Moon Sign Scorpio*

The Moon in your solar third house assists you to free yourself up from a few obligations, and it encourages a noisier Virgo than usual. In particularly this is an ideal time to express your emotions and to whisper words of love in the right ear. As the week advances, you can become more and more certain of your actions.

119

30 THURSDAY   *Moon Age Day 8   Moon Sign Scorpio*

The Sun is now in your solar third house, the herald of what happens to you towards the end of August, when it moves into your first house. For now you have the chance of a slightly quieter, more contemplative time when you may be less inclined to force issues. You might notice this more as the days go by, but this can be a useful time.

31 FRIDAY   *Moon Age Day 9   Moon Sign Sagittarius*

Another day to avoid pushing yourself or issues more than is necessary. All the same, your capacity for solid, hard work knows no bounds. There are few calls on your time that can't be used to improve your lot in life in some way, and you might decide to let certain obligations slip into the background. Why not seek attention from friends?

August
2009

1 SATURDAY
Moon Age Day 10   Moon Sign Sagittarius

Unexpected delays could well be the hallmark of this particular weekend, but you can at least make sure that what replaces your expectations is more exciting and even more productive. You can't judge any book by its binding right now, and you need to remain alert and open to new possibilities. Be prepared to spend time with loved ones.

2 SUNDAY
Moon Age Day 11   Moon Sign Sagittarius

Social trends look enlivening, and it's worth getting out there and doing something today. A few surprises are still possible, and you have what it takes to get things to line up for you – particularly if you make use of the good offices of other people. Slight delays could occur, but if you aren't in a rush today it may not matter.

3 MONDAY
Moon Age Day 12   Moon Sign Capricorn

If everything you undertake at the moment is working out pretty much the way you would wish, this probably isn't happening as a result of good luck. Rather it is thanks to the advanced planning you did some time ago, and also reflects your own positive state of mind right now. Romance is in the spotlight.

4 TUESDAY
Moon Age Day 13   Moon Sign Capricorn

One of your greatest assets at any time is your natural curiosity, and this could really come into its own today. Communication and information in equal quantity are what matter right now, and you have scope to learn new things that you can use to help you in the days to come. No stone is too small for you to turn over today.

5 WEDNESDAY   *Moon Age Day 14   Moon Sign Aquarius*

The smooth running of everyday life is probably something that appeals to you, and even when you need change and adventure you don't always welcome them. You can use today to make sure that things are working out as you expect and to gain a thorough understanding of what is needed in order to get ahead.

6 THURSDAY   *Moon Age Day 15   Moon Sign Aquarius*

Compromises at work might be more difficult to achieve today, particularly if the way others are behaving is less than ideal. As a result it's worth being somewhat careful in your approach to people and situations. The same does not hold true once work is out of the way, because social trends remain positive.

7 FRIDAY   *Moon Age Day 16   Moon Sign Aquarius*

Today could be ruled by romance – that is, if you were not a practically minded son or daughter of Virgo. Still, you have what it takes to attract a great deal of positive attention, and if you have been looking for a new relationship this is as good a time as any to get things moving. Emotions may be strong, but are often under lock and key.

8 SATURDAY   *Moon Age Day 17   Moon Sign Pisces*

Pressing ahead with certain ambitions could be difficult whilst the lunar low is around, and your best approach today is to take a well-earned rest. This might not appeal too much, particularly if you are aware that things need to be done and that they won't happen at all without your intervention. How wrong you could be!

9 SUNDAY   *Moon Age Day 18   Moon Sign Pisces*

Good judgement on your part could be somewhat lacking, but once again this is only a short response to the position of the Moon in your solar chart. If you are in any doubt, you have the option to ask for help, even if you don't really want to do so. But there is no harm whatsoever in calling in a few favours to help you clear your path.

10 MONDAY
Moon Age Day 19   Moon Sign Aries

You could somehow feel alienated from the world and a little limited by some of the pressures it seems to place upon you. This is a temporary phase brought about by the Sun in your solar twelfth house. Today responds best if you stop and think through situations, though this could bring a feeling that you are losing momentum.

11 TUESDAY
Moon Age Day 20   Moon Sign Aries

Trends enhance your winning ways, and if you make sure you are approachable and humble at the moment you can persuade all sorts of people to help you out. Don't be too quick to take offence over a disagreement with a colleague or friend. Instead, consider that what they are trying to tell you may be for your own good in the end.

12 WEDNESDAY
Moon Age Day 21   Moon Sign Aries

There is a series of great opportunities to broaden your horizons today, and with better trends on offer, you can afford to feel rather more optimistic about life generally. All mental pursuits are now well accented, and advancement is possible at work if you make sure your skills are noticed and admired by others.

13 THURSDAY
Moon Age Day 22   Moon Sign Taurus

There is little doubt that it is your inner mind that matters the most for the moment. Although you can still make satisfactory progress in your life generally, you can also take advantage of a more thoughtful interlude to spend time mulling things over. This phase is quite natural and even necessary, so there is no need to be restless.

14 FRIDAY
Moon Age Day 23   Moon Sign Taurus

A major push is now available from the planet Mars, and all of a sudden you might barely have a moment to draw breath. Be prepared to deal with the demands of others, and to sort out anything that has been waiting in the wings for a while. It's worth seeking support and practical assistance from colleagues and friends.

15 SATURDAY *Moon Age Day 24 Moon Sign Gemini*

This has potential to be one of the best days of the month for career developments – so it's something of a pity that it arrives on a Saturday when many of you will not be at work. In a social sense you can afford to go with the flow, though you should avoid sitting around waiting this weekend. The time for action has arrived!

16 SUNDAY *Moon Age Day 25 Moon Sign Gemini*

In a practical sense you have what it takes to get things done quickly and efficiently, though complete satisfaction with your lot may not be possible for another four or five days. It's difficult to be comfortable with the Sun in your twelfth house, because on the one hand it encourages restlessness, whilst on the other it urges you to think.

17 MONDAY *Moon Age Day 26 Moon Sign Cancer*

There is much to be said for paying more attention to your inner self, whilst allowing more practical aspects of life to look after themselves for a day or two. The Moon is doing you few favours right now, and it supports a more contemplative interlude when you may be less inclined to involve yourself in new projects.

18 TUESDAY *Moon Age Day 27 Moon Sign Cancer*

An ideal day to make the most of your friends and the help you can persuade them to give you. Not that you will necessarily need their assistance from a practical point of view. Your strength also lies in your ability to make progress through your own efforts, and to turn many situations in your favour.

19 WEDNESDAY *Moon Age Day 28 Moon Sign Leo*

Professionally speaking you can now make gains as a result of any job that needs your particular touch. Once you have committed yourself to something you shouldn't give in, and spending time sorting out details is a feature of your zodiac sign. Even if others see you as stubborn today, you needn't let that get in your way.

20 THURSDAY   *Moon Age Day 0   Moon Sign Leo*

Beware of jumping into things as a means of escape from situations you don't particularly like the look of. Better by far at the moment to face up to the realities of life. If you decide to do so, you'll have a chance to sort out any immediate issues. In a day or two you can take a far more optimistic view than your present outlook.

21 FRIDAY   *Moon Age Day 1   Moon Sign Virgo*

The lunar high offers scope to enjoy the first flush of a new way of dealing with life. Not only should you be more adventurous and happy to push your luck, you can also afford to be much more cheerful with yourself. The more you smile, the greater is your chance of persuading people to help you do what seems most important.

22 SATURDAY   *Moon Age Day 2   Moon Sign Virgo*

Lady Luck continues to offer you her support, and you have what it takes to make this Saturday both exciting and very interesting. Even if not everyone is on your side, that shouldn't really matter. With a combination of determination and good humour there is very little that now stands in your way. Romance is well starred for later.

23 SUNDAY   *Moon Age Day 3   Moon Sign Libra*

At last the Sun has entered your solar first house, encouraging you to feel better about yourself and your life generally. This is your time, and a period when things can be made to go your way. Don't be afraid to use your forceful and dynamic personality to impress everyone you meet.

24 MONDAY   *Moon Age Day 4   Moon Sign Libra*

Social and group relationships help you to put a smile on your face today, and you have what it takes to get ahead, especially at work. Your powers of reason are emphasised, assisting you to sort out complicated details that might have other people in a real spin. When it matters most you can come up with some very good ideas.

25 TUESDAY *Moon Age Day 5   Moon Sign Scorpio*

Virgo is a perpetual student, and you never learn enough about life to consider yourself an expert. Today is no exception, and offers you a chance to familiarise yourself with something new in just about every waking hour. Life offers fascinating options, allowing you to bring a breath of fresh air to the most stultified situations.

26 WEDNESDAY *Moon Age Day 6   Moon Sign Scorpio*

Now is the time to utilise your energy and make the most of this wonderful month in every way possible. If you are on holiday, so much the better because you have more opportunities to open your eyes and see what a great world it can be. In particular, trends encourage you to appreciate the nuances of nature in all its diversity.

27 THURSDAY *Moon Age Day 7   Moon Sign Scorpio*

Be prepared to be driven by the spirit of service and do all you can to lend a hand. It doesn't really matter who you help, what counts is that you feel useful and are more than willing to go that extra mile. The gratitude you can attract should be reward enough for all your efforts, and you can afford to keep smiling all day.

28 FRIDAY *Moon Age Day 8   Moon Sign Sagittarius*

When it comes to professional matters, you need to be careful not to impose your will on other people. Rather than trying to talk your way through situations, today's trends encourage you to lead by example and gain respect along the way. With the weekend ahead, it's worth planning something fascinating for yourself and your lover.

29 SATURDAY *Moon Age Day 9   Moon Sign Sagittarius*

Virgo can take advantage of a potentially good day at a personal level. Your ego and your confidence are both emphasised, and you have what it takes to make a difference. At the same time you also have very high standards, and others may well find it difficult to keep up with you. Social trends are positive.

30 SUNDAY   *Moon Age Day 10   Moon Sign Capricorn*

You can afford to remain open and sensitive to the plight of others, no matter whether they live next door or across the other side of the planet. An ideal day to do what you can to help, particularly by using your practical skills to find positive ways to make a difference. Make the most of new encounters with people you haven't seen for ages.

31 MONDAY   *Moon Age Day 11   Moon Sign Capricorn*

Material matters are now much enhanced, so it makes sense to remain enterprising in your outlook. By all means take more of a chance from a financial point of view, but make sure any risks you do take are calculated ones. There should now be little to stand in your way, though you may decide to relax rather than work too hard.

♍ September

2009

1 TUESDAY
Moon Age Day 12   Moon Sign Capricorn

The first day of September heralds a risk of minor conflicts and puts the spotlight on the more argumentative side of your nature. The danger is greatest if you think your integrity is under attack, even if nothing is further from the truth. You needn't defend yourself so much – particularly if nobody is threatening you!

2 WEDNESDAY
Moon Age Day 13   Moon Sign Aquarius

You can make the most of what today offers by being busy and fulfilled in your daily life. Feeling useful is also very important, and you have what it takes to turn your hand to almost anything. Creature comforts might be more significant towards the evening, though if the Sun shines you might choose to take a break earlier on.

3 THURSDAY
Moon Age Day 14   Moon Sign Aquarius

Enthusiasm for relationships could be slightly lacking with Venus now occupying your solar twelfth house. This may well only strike home in the case of people you don't know very well. Trends encourage a tendency for you to mistrust others and to believe they are working against your best interests. Could you be wrong?

4 FRIDAY
Moon Age Day 15   Moon Sign Pisces

Your best approach is to keep your life as simple as possible while the lunar low is around. Beware of taking on more than you have to, and rest whenever you get the chance. If it's been hectic recently, you deserve to relax for a while. Any minor frustrations caused by family relationships should be easy to deal with.

5 SATURDAY
Moon Age Day 16   Moon Sign Pisces

Slight disruptions to your everyday life are still possible, but once again these come as phantoms rather than anything with a tangible shape. The lunar low supports a tendency to worry about issues that are not in the least important and to be rather too fussy for your own good. By tomorrow you can make sure that things look better.

6 SUNDAY
Moon Age Day 17   Moon Sign Pisces

As the lunar low fades, you have scope to make important changes in your life, though it pays to be ready to think through your plans again if things comes unstuck. There isn't really any way to avoid this, but since you are so good at thinking on your feet there should be no real problem. Why not seek support from your partner?

7 MONDAY
☿   *Moon Age Day 18   Moon Sign Aries*

You can now capitalise on exciting possibilities and an interlude during which what you want and what you can achieve could be more or less the same thing. The urge to create is heightened, and with the Sun still in your solar first house you have scope to push forward on all fronts. It's worth seeking support from relatives.

8 TUESDAY
☿   *Moon Age Day 19   Moon Sign Aries*

Many Virgo subjects may well decide to reserve today for love. Trends encourage romantic feelings, and assist you to elicit a positive response from that someone special in your life. In a more practical sense, even if it takes you a while to get going this morning, once you do you can get most aspects of life going your way.

9 WEDNESDAY
☿   *Moon Age Day 20   Moon Sign Taurus*

Some conflict could arise within your social circle, and though you many not be the one who is promoting it, your strength lies in being able to sort things out. You have a tremendous knack for getting inside the minds of other people and for understanding what makes them tick. There are gains to be made by using your intuition to the full.

129

10 THURSDAY ☿ *Moon Age Day 21 Moon Sign Taurus*

The time is now right to follow your intuition where money is concerned. You can be as informed as you like, but at the end of the day it will be gut reactions that guide you the best. Not everyone might accept your point of view, and as a result you could get quite frustrated. Rather than losing your temper, why not simply smile?

11 FRIDAY ☿ *Moon Age Day 22 Moon Sign Gemini*

Make the most of a potentially buoyant phase as your energies and spirits are enhanced. Even if others think everything is going wrong, you have what it takes to come in and sort things out. From a social and a romantic point of view you should be riding high, though fortune may not be smiling on you in the financial stakes.

12 SATURDAY ☿ *Moon Age Day 23 Moon Sign Gemini*

Your expectations of others, and indeed yourself, will be best kept to a minimum today. This is because Venus still occupies your solar twelfth house, and does little to help your progress. What is available today is the chance to discuss things in a serious manner and to come to some quite surprising conclusions as a result.

13 SUNDAY ☿ *Moon Age Day 24 Moon Sign Cancer*

You may well decide to extricate yourself from social commitments today, particularly if you just don't feel like becoming involved, and also on account of your present need to fly solo for at least some of the time. Routines might get in the way of personal enjoyment for part of today, but a few tasks can simply be left until later.

14 MONDAY ☿ *Moon Age Day 25 Moon Sign Cancer*

Today can be great from a personal point of view, but there is a definite contest in your life between the influence of the Sun and of Venus. Getting your own way shouldn't be too difficult, though there may be moments when you come up against people who simply will not give way, even if you know they are wrong.

15 TUESDAY ☿ *Moon Age Day 26   Moon Sign Leo*

This is a time of potential spiritual growth and of increased creative potential. Prepare to take advantage of these trends by considering your surroundings and giving thought to any alterations that will make you more comfortable in the months ahead. Your energy and commitment are emphasised right now.

16 WEDNESDAY ☿ *Moon Age Day 27   Moon Sign Leo*

Today is an ideal time for strong emotional commitment and for making the most of interludes during which you can gain affection from both expected and unexpected directions. It could be that you have an admirer you never even suspected, and though this can be gratifying and touching it could be embarrassing too.

17 THURSDAY ☿ *Moon Age Day 28   Moon Sign Virgo*

The Moon returns to your zodiac sign, and with it comes a strong practical boost, together with a more carefree attitude. If you keep your confidence high, there shouldn't be much to get in your way, especially at work. When the day's commitments are out of the way, you can afford to turn your mind towards love.

18 FRIDAY ☿ *Moon Age Day 29   Moon Sign Virgo*

Today favours change and personal growth in all departments of your life. With a strong commitment to others you can show yourself to be both capable and caring. There are some very rewarding experiences on offer, and though you may have to look hard for them the effort should be worthwhile. Finances are well starred.

19 SATURDAY ☿ *Moon Age Day 0   Moon Sign Virgo*

The lunar high assists you to express yourself this weekend, and you can derive a great deal of joy from simply talking to people. This is a favourable time for getting involved in community projects and showing how charity-minded you can be at the moment. Strong social impulses help you to move towards new possibilities.

131

20 SUNDAY ☿ *Moon Age Day 1   Moon Sign Libra*

A few personal sacrifices may now be necessary if you are to have a chance of achieving rewarding results for both you and for those you care for. Today is a time of significant commitment and a period when you need to recognise your responsibilities to the full. Personal rewards are there for the taking.

21 MONDAY ☿ *Moon Age Day 2   Moon Sign Libra*

It is very important now that you stay as well informed as proves to be possible. This is not a time to be going out on a limb or to be taking chances with important matters. Virgo is inclined to take life fairly seriously on occasions, and this could well be the case at the start of this week. Laughter may be hard to find at present.

22 TUESDAY ☿ *Moon Age Day 3   Moon Sign Scorpio*

You still have what it takes to be busy – but then there is nothing remotely strange about that. With Mercury in a good position, you can use your mental processes to impress others and to benefit yourself as well. It is towards the material aspects of life that trends now encourage your mind to turn the most.

23 WEDNESDAY ☿ *Moon Age Day 4   Moon Sign Scorpio*

At long last Venus has moved from your solar twelfth house and into your first. Good things can be achieved as a result if you take time to express yourself and focus your attention on the love that surrounds you. You are now in a position to find out more about help you have been given by others recently.

24 THURSDAY ☿ *Moon Age Day 5   Moon Sign Sagittarius*

It would be best if you were to take methodical steps right now, and you need to avoid rushing your fences in almost everything. Don't be afraid to mull over new ideas as much as proves to be necessary, and don't be rushed. At work you have scope to show how capable you can be, even if you aren't getting the accolades you really deserve.

25 FRIDAY ☿ *Moon Age Day 6   Moon Sign Sagittarius*

Today your deeply emotional nature is highlighted. This could manifest itself in you being moved to tears by the plight of others, even those who are at a distance. You may even decide to offer practical help. Where possible now it's worth concentrating on domestic matters and on making changes in and around your home.

26 SATURDAY ☿ *Moon Age Day 7   Moon Sign Capricorn*

Romantic matters seem to be your forte, and you can use this influence to attract some particularly interesting company. An active approach works best during most of the weekend, so sticking around at home may not be ideal. Why not invite your partners and like-minded friends to do something different and fascinating?

27 SUNDAY ☿ *Moon Age Day 8   Moon Sign Capricorn*

With Venus now in your own zodiac sign you are encouraged to express both charm and grace in your dealings with the world at large. This is a chance to show how warm and interesting you can be, whilst also expressing yourself in a very positive sort of way. You have real potential to make this a red-letter day.

28 MONDAY ☿ *Moon Age Day 9   Moon Sign Capricorn*

Now you can make sure the pace of life is swift and also pleasurable. In addition to Venus you now have Mercury in your solar first house, and Mercury is your ruling planet. Capitalise on the pieces of useful information you can discover, some of it from fairly unexpected directions, and make use of the help you can obtain.

29 TUESDAY ☿ *Moon Age Day 10   Moon Sign Aquarius*

An ideal time to bring minor matters to a satisfactory conclusion, though the happiness you feel as a result may be out of all proportion to what you have achieved. Negotiations are well accented under present influences, and you have what it takes to bring others round to your specific point of view.

30 WEDNESDAY ☿ *Moon Age Day 11   Moon Sign Aquarius*

Getting your own way at the moment is a matter of charm and coercion. It's possible that you could be slightly underhand in some of your dealings, but you can justify this if the result benefits others too. Not everyone can face up to the truth, and a little subterfuge is right up Virgo's street when it proves to be absolutely necessary.

October

2009

1 THURSDAY
Moon Age Day 12   Moon Sign Pisces

It's the first day of October, and with a new month comes the lunar low, which you will have to deal with as best you can. Be prepared to deal with unexpected situations, and to exercise care about taking on new challenges or extra responsibilities. You certainly needn't be tardy when it comes to expressing love!

2 FRIDAY
Moon Age Day 13   Moon Sign Pisces

You may decide that some plans will have to wait until later. Even if the lunar low is not very potent this time around, it can take the wind out of your sails somewhat. Try not to get stuck into too much of a rut, though it has to be said that making startling progress may not be easy. This has all the hallmarks of a very average sort of day.

3 SATURDAY
Moon Age Day 14   Moon Sign Pisces

You have scope to change things as soon as today dawns, particularly if you turn your mind away from work and towards more social and romantic possibilities. Venus in its present position assists you to express your emotions, and today also offers you a chance to come face to face with individuals who can be of great use to you.

4 SUNDAY
Moon Age Day 15   Moon Sign Aries

When it comes to problem solving, you should be right on the ball today. Almost any sort of puzzle appeals to you, and you also have what it takes to sort it out in a flash. This is just as true in a practical sense as it would be in the case of a newspaper crossword. It doesn't matter how much of a mess others are in – you can find the solution.

5 MONDAY
Moon Age Day 16   Moon Sign Aries

When it comes to your social life you can create a powerful impression right now and make sure that people notice your presence. Friends and colleagues should appreciate the fact that you are forthright and that they know exactly how you feel about situations. Bear in mind that others might find you a little pushy.

6 TUESDAY
Moon Age Day 17   Moon Sign Taurus

In a general sense you can now make steady progress, but can make the most of a fortunate interlude when it comes to money. By all means strengthen your finances as a result of careful speculation, though it's not worth pushing your luck more than you know is sensible. At the end of the day yours is a very careful zodiac sign.

7 WEDNESDAY
Moon Age Day 18   Moon Sign Taurus

You can use meetings with others to inspire you with new ideas and to feed your intellect no end. If you have the sort of job that brings you into contact with the world at large, so much the better. As far as your personal life is concerned, you can afford to feel happy with your lot, even if certain other people are not.

8 THURSDAY
Moon Age Day 19   Moon Sign Gemini

Now is the time to gain a distinct advantage over anyone you count as being a competitor. You shouldn't have to be ruthless to get ahead, particularly if you base your progress on consistency and your willingness to keep going when others fall by the wayside. In the end you have what it takes to prove yourself time and again.

9 FRIDAY
Moon Age Day 20   Moon Sign Gemini

What seems to matter the most today is your ability to communicate with friends and family members. As far as your partner is concerned, it appears you now have scope to explain yourself much better than was the case over the last couple of days. The focus is now on pleasing that most important person in your life.

10 SATURDAY   *Moon Age Day 21   Moon Sign Gemini*

Since Venus is still in your solar first house, as is Mercury, the fun-loving side of your nature should never be very far from the surface. Trends encourage you to show how funny you can be, and if there are pranks being played at the moment, there are signs that you are the chief culprit. Whatever you choose to do today, do it with style!

11 SUNDAY   *Moon Age Day 22   Moon Sign Cancer*

Prevailing influences continue to put the spotlight on material issues, and you should be doing all you can to make sure that the months ahead are positive, especially from a financial point of view. As far as today is concerned, don't be afraid to put petty worries or irritations firmly on the back burner.

12 MONDAY   *Moon Age Day 23   Moon Sign Cancer*

The Moon has entered a part of your chart that is not quite so favourable for winning out over competition, so you may decide it is sensible not to try today. This is a time when you would be best served by watching and waiting. That doesn't mean the day has to be short of interest, but merely that you can afford to make slower progress.

13 TUESDAY   *Moon Age Day 24   Moon Sign Leo*

Instead of moving in the direction of others, you now have what it takes to bring them to you. You may well be a little less inclined to travel or to seek out new places, and you can take this opportunity to sit for a little while at the centre of your own web. Be prepared to address the distinct needs that people have of you.

14 WEDNESDAY   *Moon Age Day 25   Moon Sign Leo*

In another day or so you can change almost everything, but for now it's worth being fairly circumspect and not taking on any more than you know you can successfully handle. Even if you are still working hard, it's possible that a part of your nature wants to retreat, and it might be rather difficult to concentrate as much as usual.

15 THURSDAY
Moon Age Day 26   Moon Sign Virgo

The lunar high assists you to perk things up, and offers you everything you need to get on well with any project that is important to you. An ideal day to seek happiness in the company of others, and to make the most of their support. Wearing a smile on your face all day can certainly help you to work wonders.

16 FRIDAY
Moon Age Day 27   Moon Sign Virgo

Generally speaking your luck is emphasised, though even under the lunar high there are still places that don't offer you the best opportunities to increase your fortunes. Be prepared to use your enhanced intuition to recognise these places. Romance and loving attachments are well marked under present influences.

17 SATURDAY
Moon Age Day 28   Moon Sign Libra

What seems to be most important at the moment is consolidating your position in a general sense. Material securities should be in better shape than they have been for quite a while, though a great deal of this has to do with your present attitude. In other words, it's possible that nothing much has changed except the way you view your life.

18 SUNDAY
Moon Age Day 0   Moon Sign Libra

You are now in a position to make financial progress, even to the extent that you might be looking at the possibility of a part-time job or some form of speculation that looks as though it could pay off. Beware of falling for get-rich-quick schemes, though being a Virgo subject someone would have to be very good to fool you.

19 MONDAY
Moon Age Day 1   Moon Sign Scorpio

An ideal day to strengthen your finances even more, and to look very seriously at improving your lifestyle in some way. Trends now encourage Virgo towards luxury, and it's worth finding moments today when you can positively revel in the chance to spoil yourself. The only slight drawback is that to do so might cost you something.

20 TUESDAY   *Moon Age Day 2   Moon Sign Scorpio*

Getting together in discussion with colleagues and friends can now be used to your distinct advantage, even if there are people involved that you don't particularly like. Who knows? With a little patience and perseverance on your part you could get to know a former adversary better and end up liking them a great deal.

21 WEDNESDAY   *Moon Age Day 3   Moon Sign Sagittarius*

The focus now turns to domestic matters, and the present position of the Moon assists your involvement in family concerns to a greater extent. If you have more time on your hands, you can afford to put yourself out in order to please your nearest and dearest, though having started this process it might be difficult to stop!

22 THURSDAY   *Moon Age Day 4   Moon Sign Sagittarius*

Close ties are potentially your most rewarding area today, so be prepared to turn on the charm in order to please the most important person in your life. Emotions may well run close to the surface, and you have scope to speak your mind to a greater extent when it comes to expressing your true feelings.

23 FRIDAY   *Moon Age Day 5   Moon Sign Sagittarius*

The impact of your personality is now highlighted, and you can use this to make sure you are not ignored by anyone today. The practical side of life is a different matter, and you could well be soon bored by the sort of routines you generally take in your stride. A day to play to win in any form of competition, and to be quite ruthless.

24 SATURDAY   *Moon Age Day 6   Moon Sign Capricorn*

The Sun has now entered your solar third house, assisting you to create a favourable impression on practically everyone you meet. This is particularly the case if you give a good account of yourself and if you make full use of your charms when in company. Instead of simply being intelligent, you now have an opportunity to show the fact.

25 SUNDAY   *Moon Age Day 7   Moon Sign Capricorn*

There is still a tendency for you to spend more money on indulgences than you would as a rule. At the same time you have scope to make financial gains, so you can ensure that your overall bank balance doesn't change very much. This is a good time to enhance your physical surroundings and to make relatives more comfortable too.

26 MONDAY   *Moon Age Day 8   Moon Sign Aquarius*

Trends highlight a strong sense of urgency and a desire on your part to bring to a close issues you think have been going on for too long. You should be able to look closely at the most minute details and get things right in most areas of your life. If there is a problem here, it lies in the fact that certain people may not understand you.

27 TUESDAY   *Moon Age Day 9   Moon Sign Aquarius*

Current trends definitely favour information gathering, and your strength lies in not leaving a single stone unturned on the path of your life. This stands you in good stead and helps you to glean important details. If you want to keep up your exacting approach, you may have to work on your own, because others can't keep up!

28 WEDNESDAY   *Moon Age Day 10   Moon Sign Aquarius*

Don't be afraid to follow your heart today, and choose your words carefully when you are addressing matters of love. There are ways in which you can please those around you, whilst at the same time feathering your own nest, and although you might feel guilty about the fact, why should you? Everyone has a chance to be happy.

29 THURSDAY   *Moon Age Day 11   Moon Sign Pisces*

Don't be surprised if you have to overturn some of your plans today. The lunar low is around, supporting a more careful approach than usual. It doesn't matter how long it takes you to do things today because what is important is that they are done properly. Moving ahead in leaps and bounds probably won't be top of your list for now

30 FRIDAY
Moon Age Day 12   Moon Sign Pisces

If general energy levels are low, the best way of getting exactly what you want today is to persuade others to take some of the strain. This may not be a situation that will please you at all, particularly if you really would love to be in command. What is more, it might be hard to trust others to sort things out in quite the way you would.

31 SATURDAY
Moon Age Day 13   Moon Sign Aries

You can make the most of a better period on the financial front, and can make sure any difficulties caused by the lunar low disappear like the morning mist. You have scope to get more of what you want and to gain the help of your partner to do this. You can also use the support of willing family members to boost your success.

November

2009

1 SUNDAY
Moon Age Day 14   Moon Sign Aries

The first day of November offers the chance of even swifter progress, and a realisation that you can get things going your way as far as the practicalities of life are concerned. Care is still necessary, though you can finally put paid to recent delays and positively cruise along. This probably won't be a day for social niceties.

2 MONDAY
Moon Age Day 15   Moon Sign Aries

Frequent excursions are the order of the day, and for those Virgo subjects who have decided to take a late holiday the choice will prove to have been very fortuitous indeed. A great many situations can now be sorted out, leaving you with more time to explore possibilities that haven't occurred to you before.

3 TUESDAY
Moon Age Day 16   Moon Sign Taurus

Even if you continue to make progress in a general sense, trends suggest that you might be more easily distracted at the moment. Confidence remains generally high, but if you don't concentrate as much as usual, errors are possible. Your creative potential is emphasised, and some people would call you ingenious now!

4 WEDNESDAY
Moon Age Day 17   Moon Sign Taurus

The pleasure principle is strong, encouraging a slight tendency for you to spend too much and to become too fond of luxury. It has to be remembered that yours is an Earth sign, and this alone means that you can be something of a hedonist. Try a spoonful of moderation, though it is a medicine you probably won't care for today.

5 THURSDAY   *Moon Age Day 18   Moon Sign Gemini*

Enjoying the thrill of the chase is no bad thing, especially when it comes to romance. A word of warning to some Virgo subjects though: you can become so committed to the conquest that you forget about the nature of the prize. Beware of trying to make someone love you deeply unless you are sure you care for them in return.

6 FRIDAY   *Moon Age Day 19   Moon Sign Gemini*

You can reap the greatest benefits today through teamwork and your ability to make everyone around you feel as though they are indispensable. The kindest and most considerate side of Virgo can now be displayed, and it is a side that is very popular. You shouldn't forget a kindness today and can afford to repay each one handsomely.

7 SATURDAY   *Moon Age Day 20   Moon Sign Cancer*

The focus is on a feeling of extravagance, and this is because Venus has now moved into your solar second house. This encourages you to spend money on things you don't really need, and also to overindulge in a number of different ways. Make the most of your current earning powers in order to avoid a deficit.

8 SUNDAY   *Moon Age Day 21   Moon Sign Cancer*

Mercury in your solar third house enhances your thinking power and assists you to be direct when it comes to sorting out tricky problems. Now is the time to seek out situations that test your skills and even stretch the bounds of what you once thought was possible. Your fineness of touch is also noteworthy under these trends.

9 MONDAY   *Moon Age Day 22   Moon Sign Leo*

A little versatility is what you require today, and you can use it to pursue your desire to get ahead. You can also use a number of talents you didn't know you had, though a few obstacles on the path to success are possible too. At some stage during the day it's worth finding moments that are exclusively your own.

10 TUESDAY   *Moon Age Day 23   Moon Sign Leo*

If progress is far from dynamic, for that you can thank a twelfth-house Moon. All the same there are gains to be made, though these may be low-key and also probably quite private in nature. Get yourself into the mood for action and clear the decks, because for the next couple of days you have a chance to make things go your way.

11 WEDNESDAY   *Moon Age Day 24   Moon Sign Virgo*

If ever there was an opportunity for you to tempt fate, today is the day you should notice it the most. The lunar high allows you to move closer to some of your heart's desires, though not as a result of simple good fortune. If you know what you want from life you should have very little trouble getting it. Finances are well marked.

12 THURSDAY   *Moon Age Day 25   Moon Sign Virgo*

You have what it takes to get your own way today, partly if you make sure others recognise your talents, but also if you refuse to take no for an answer. Look out for an unexpected opportunity to change your surroundings in some way. It could be that there is an offer of travel, or simply that you want to shake up your routines.

13 FRIDAY   *Moon Age Day 26   Moon Sign Libra*

The present position of Mars supports a slightly short-tempered interlude, and you may be inclined to fly off the handle without any real justification. Be open and honest with loved ones and don't get into a muddle over issues that can easily be addressed. Patience is in short supply, and that could be the major drawback now.

14 SATURDAY   *Moon Age Day 27   Moon Sign Libra*

Present planetary influences bring out the best in you when it comes to communicating with the world at large. You have scope to get in touch with as many people as possible and should use every means at your disposal to make sure you are in the know. Listen out, because the most unlikely comments can prove to be helpful.

15 SUNDAY   *Moon Age Day 28   Moon Sign Scorpio*

You should still be on top form and well able to use hidden advantages to improve your lot in life. It won't have escaped your attention that the year is growing older, and there is much to be said for looking to see how many of your plans for this year have paid off. You might decide on a final push where some of them are concerned.

16 MONDAY   *Moon Age Day 29   Moon Sign Scorpio*

An ideal day for exchanging ideas with others and talking as much as possible to individuals who have it in their power to help you along. Rather than getting tied down with pointless routines, why not keep your schedules open for 'instant' happenings? Being flexible counts for a great deal at this time.

17 TUESDAY   *Moon Age Day 0   Moon Sign Scorpio*

Some responsibilities require a great deal of mental discipline, and this is when you can really come into your own. Whilst others dilly-dally around, you have what it takes to work things out instantly. Use this ability to get yourself to the front of any queue and to ensure that people in authority notice your presence.

18 WEDNESDAY   *Moon Age Day 1   Moon Sign Sagittarius*

Trends suggest that family interests are very much to the fore today. There are good reasons to focus your attention on making sure those you love are comfortable and have whatever they need. In your own life you now have a chance to discover the importance of having a place for everything and a plan for each contingency.

19 THURSDAY   *Moon Age Day 2   Moon Sign Sagittarius*

Make the most of today's positive conditions by choosing to rub shoulders with people to whom you take an instant liking. Of course you can't be fond of everyone, and there could be the odd person about who seems committed to messing you about. Fortunately you have the ability to smile and carry on without reacting.

20 FRIDAY   *Moon Age Day 3   Moon Sign Capricorn*

You have scope to appreciate the emotional responses of others today and to put yourself in the market for romance. Showing commitment to your partner – or maybe someone you wish was your partner – should encourage a positive response. Finances are well accented too, and there could be a chance to gain cash that you didn't expect.

21 SATURDAY   *Moon Age Day 4   Moon Sign Capricorn*

You might benefit from a retreat of some sort today. You need to raise inspiration within yourself, and that might mean having to stop moving forward in specific instances in order to move forward more progressively later. At least you needn't be slow when it comes to accepting social invitations or romantic offers.

22 SUNDAY   *Moon Age Day 5   Moon Sign Capricorn*

Current trends support smooth sailing in all negotiations and discussions with family and friends. Even if attention to detail isn't all you would wish, that shouldn't really matter because most of the details of life could sort themselves out. You have scope to get on particularly well at the moment with people you see as being efficient.

23 MONDAY   *Moon Age Day 6   Moon Sign Aquarius*

You may now decide to take life a little easier and might be willing to take more rest than has been the case in recent days. The spotlight is on a great desire to somehow improve your home life, and to put work considerations on the back burner as a result. It is important to feed your intellect in every way possible around this time.

24 TUESDAY   *Moon Age Day 7   Moon Sign Aquarius*

Today's planetary emphasis assists you to make a smooth ride of work and practical affairs. Once again it's worth checking that you are well up to date and that others are willing to do their bit. All in all you can take advantage of a fairly easy-going interlude and a time when you can really discover the meaning of the word 'relax'!

YOUR DAILY GUIDE TO NOVEMBER 2009

25 WEDNESDAY   *Moon Age Day 8   Moon Sign Pisces*

Progress isn't just steady today and tomorrow, it might seem to have stopped altogether. Even if this isn't what you had bargained for, a realisation that the lunar low is around can help you to feel slightly better about things generally. Probably the most important factor when considering the slow-down is that you don't really care.

26 THURSDAY   *Moon Age Day 9   Moon Sign Pisces*

The lunar low supports a feeling of being in the dark regarding a particular plan of action and of being left out of negotiations that have a great part to play in your future. Once again you need to be careful before you react harshly. Things are not what they seem and it would be all too easy to go off half-cock, without thinking first.

27 FRIDAY   *Moon Age Day 10   Moon Sign Pisces*

Your best approach is to move forward slowly and steadily, though only in very specific directions. Even if others aren't doing what they should, you probably won't yet be in a position to do much about the fact. By tomorrow the lunar low is out of the way and you can then make the most of a much more progressive phase.

28 SATURDAY   *Moon Age Day 11   Moon Sign Aries*

It might seem as though your general popularity has reached its peak, leaving you feeling as though you don't have the level of influence in the world at large that you did only a week or so ago. Actually nothing much has changed, except your own point of view. Why not concentrate on specific tasks today and tomorrow?

29 SUNDAY   *Moon Age Day 12   Moon Sign Aries*

It's time to realise that November is drawing to a close and that the holiday season will soon be upon you. As a result you could be indulging in some ferocious shopping excursions, and woe betide anyone who decides to go along with you. Energy is something you probably don't lack, but can the world keep up?

147

30 MONDAY
Moon Age Day 13   Moon Sign Taurus

It is on domestic matters that you are encouraged to spend much of
your thinking time at the start of this week. Even if you are still busy
at work, you have what it takes to get things done in half the usual
time, leaving you more time to consider other matters. Once you
have made up your mind, don't be afraid to stick to it this week.

♍

December

2009

1 TUESDAY   *Moon Age Day 14   Moon Sign Taurus*

Trends assist you to show your natural diplomacy at this time, and you can use it to get almost anyone to follow your lead. This is achieved with just a dash of bullying and a great deal of encouragement. By all means take a middle path between warring parties, but beware of getting personally involved.

2 WEDNESDAY   *Moon Age Day 15   Moon Sign Gemini*

Although you do want to make compromises as much as proves to be possible, there are occasions today when this may not be an option. You usually know how you feel about specific situations, though you are now less inclined to be so positive. Jumping about from foot to foot is a strange experience for Virgo.

3 THURSDAY   *Moon Age Day 16   Moon Sign Gemini*

Good luck can help you to achieve some of your objectives, whilst others are accomplished through your ability to focus and to work hard. Merely agreeing or disagreeing with those around you won't be enough today, because your strength lies in taking the lead in most areas of life. You can persuade people to trust you now.

4 FRIDAY   *Moon Age Day 17   Moon Sign Cancer*

The Sun is now in your solar fourth house and in this position it enhances your sense of your responsibilities, especially regarding home and family. An active and enterprising Virgo is fine for the world at large, but at home a more circumspect approach may be called for, especially if you need to support someone else.

149

5 SATURDAY
Moon Age Day 18   Moon Sign Cancer

The most advantageous and rewarding experiences are still those that you create when you are at home. The world outside your door may not look quite so appealing this weekend, particularly if you are in the full throws of preparing for the upcoming Christmas period. Nostalgia reigns as you get out the decorations!

6 SUNDAY
Moon Age Day 19   Moon Sign Leo

There is now a definite focus on personal self-expression. It will be of great importance to you not merely to say how you feel but to explain yourself fully. For Virgo this is usually easy because you communicate very well. However, there might be complications if you have to express the true nature of your inner emotions.

7 MONDAY
Moon Age Day 20   Moon Sign Leo

Disputes are possible today, particularly if the desires of others clash somewhat with your own needs and wants. Your best response is to use your persuasive powers, which are emphasised at the moment, to get your own way. Work issues could seem like heavy demands, but you can make sure the rest of the week is less stressed.

8 TUESDAY
Moon Age Day 21   Moon Sign Virgo

You can capitalise on a potentially good time today and tomorrow. The lunar high assists you to be on top form and anxious to enjoy yourself, no matter what you happen to be doing. Put your best foot forward and do all that is necessary to make life better and easier. You have what it takes to strengthen your finances now.

9 WEDNESDAY
Moon Age Day 22   Moon Sign Virgo

This is a favourable time for luck and personal growth. In quite a few ways the world should be opening up to you, and the chance of you gaining ground at work especially is particularly strong. There are new gifts and blessings available, though some of them come in such a disguised form that it could take a while to recognise them.

10 THURSDAY
Moon Age Day 23   Moon Sign Libra

Work and professional matters are still well accented, though you could feel that extra responsibility is being placed upon you. All the same it's worth soldiering on in a very positive way and showing everyone just how keen you are to get ahead. In order to balance all this work, you need to make sure your social life is doing all it can for you.

11 FRIDAY
Moon Age Day 24   Moon Sign Libra

Now that the Sun occupies your solar fourth house, you have a chance to recognise the importance of your own private world. If you feel stressed or under pressure at work you can afford to retreat into yourself much more than you did earlier in the year. There is no harm in this, because Virgo needs periods of relative isolation.

12 SATURDAY
Moon Age Day 25   Moon Sign Libra

Not only the Sun but also Venus occupies your solar fourth house, and all these trends point to a time during which there is greater focus on house and home than of late. Perhaps this isn't surprising in any case, because Christmas is on the way. An ideal time for sorting out those seasonal arrangements.

13 SUNDAY
Moon Age Day 26   Moon Sign Scorpio

Even if you want to push on in a general sense, you would be wise to be more aware of your own limitations today, and that could mean having to rely on the good offices of those around you to a much greater extent than you normally would. There is a slight danger that you could allow your imagination to run away with you.

14 MONDAY
Moon Age Day 27   Moon Sign Scorpio

Your intellectual curiosity could well be stimulated today, encouraging you to find out what makes everything tick. There should be plenty of opportunities for you to satisfy this urge to acquire knowledge, and almost everything in life offers new lessons. Be prepared to take pleasure and joy in new personalities.

15 TUESDAY   *Moon Age Day 28   Moon Sign Sagittarius*

What a good time this would be for showing off and for convincing others that you are equal to just about any task they want to set you. From a social point of view the emphasis is on places of entertainment, and you can use this trend to make the most of pre-Christmas gatherings of all kinds.

16 WEDNESDAY   *Moon Age Day 0   Moon Sign Sagittarius*

Now is a good time to bring about changes at home, and the day of the New Moon could prove to be especially fortunate for you. Issues from the past could well revisit you, but you can ensure that this is a pleasing and reassuring experience. Nostalgia is quite acceptable at this time of year, as long as it doesn't get out of hand.

17 THURSDAY   *Moon Age Day 1   Moon Sign Capricorn*

You now respond best to a domestic atmosphere that is both warm and secure – yet another reflection of the present position of the Sun in your chart. There should be plenty of opportunity to relax and a great desire on your part to be kind to others. You have what it takes to develop that Christmas spirit ahead of time!

18 FRIDAY   *Moon Age Day 2   Moon Sign Capricorn*

You can use this as a useful period of self-examination and contemplation. Mars is now in your solar twelfth house, and this could dissuade you from being quite as committed in a professional sense as would often be the case. It wouldn't be at all surprising to discover that you don't want much at all today – except peace and quiet.

19 SATURDAY   *Moon Age Day 3   Moon Sign Capricorn*

One of the greatest saving graces in your solar chart at the moment is Mercury, which is in your solar fifth house. This supports a cheerful attitude and a willingness to accept whatever comes your way. If you are busy now, be prepared to sort out various details. Above all you would be wise to be organised today.

20 SUNDAY   *Moon Age Day 4   Moon Sign Aquarius*

Home is a great place for entertaining at the moment, and trends suggest that you can be happier there than anywhere else. Even if your level of drive is not at its highest, you can be a great host right now and have what it takes to make everyone feel at ease. Capitalise on your ability to maintain your popularity.

21 MONDAY   *Moon Age Day 5   Moon Sign Aquarius*

At work it looks as though you should be overflowing with good ideas today. This may be a direct response to the trends of withdrawal last week, and your wish to make up for the fact now. The social trends are still quite positive, but don't be surprised if you are once again taken over by more private impulses later in the day.

22 TUESDAY   *Moon Age Day 6   Moon Sign Pisces*

Stand by for a slightly sluggish period now that the lunar low has arrived. The one good thing is that you can get it out of the way before Christmas actually arrives. Be prepared to rely a great deal today on the good offices of others, and if there is something you simply cannot do, to enlist the support of a professional.

23 WEDNESDAY   *Moon Age Day 7   Moon Sign Pisces*

This is not the most suitable time to tempt fate by taking on risky propositions. Keep life steady and stick to what you know best. Grandiose schemes are best left until after Christmas, by which time you might have forgotten about them anyway. An ideal day to seek support from friends, and to get involved in their activities.

24 THURSDAY   *Moon Age Day 8   Moon Sign Pisces*

Loved ones and all social connections are favoured right now, and with Christmas Eve arriving you may suddenly realise how many things you haven't done. That doesn't matter. What counts is realising how much love surrounds you and making the most of it. You should be on good form socially towards the end of the day.

25 FRIDAY   *Moon Age Day 9   Moon Sign Aries*

This has potential to be a romantic Christmas Day par excellence for many sons and daughters of Virgo. Your commitment to that someone special is particularly strong, but you should have more than enough affection to share out among others who are close to you. Stand by to enjoy some unexpected gifts.

26 SATURDAY   *Moon Age Day 10   Moon Sign Aries*

Trends enhance your natural talent for attracting the good offices and assistance of friends, and this can be useful today. You don't need to be a stay-at-home for Boxing Day, and might be more inclined to travel about. It's not worth getting yourself into a panic, even if you have to reorganise certain things at the last minute.

27 SUNDAY   *Moon Age Day 11   Moon Sign Taurus*

The focus is on your strong desire to expand your boundaries today, particularly if you are already tiring of parties and mince pies. Getting yourself back into gear would be no bad thing, but that may not be possible until after the coming weekend. For the moment you can plan, and can also keep yourself busy with social happenings.

28 MONDAY   *Moon Age Day 12   Moon Sign Taurus*

This is a time to be on the move and to find new things to do. You could so easily get bored, and then you will be less pleasant to know than you have been for quite a few days. Why not see if you can help out someone in the family, particularly if your own particular specialities are very relevant to them? Take advantage of interesting offers.

29 TUESDAY   *Moon Age Day 13   Moon Sign Taurus*

Mars in its present position can bring a little confusion into your life, and you may find it more difficult to stick to arrangements. If you have to change your mind at the last minute, don't get upset about it. There are occasions when Virgo needs to be more flexible, and it won't do you any harm at all to be a creature of the moment.

30 WEDNESDAY   *Moon Age Day 14   Moon Sign Gemini*

Involvements in the social and romantic arena ought to prove rewarding now. Don't be afraid to get out, meet others and try new things. It's time for you to generally show off your most attractive traits to others. What's more, you have what it takes to stand in the limelight at present, without feeling in the least conspicuous.

31 THURSDAY   *Moon Age Day 15   Moon Sign Gemini*

This has potential to be a high-spirited period, with scope to increase your popularity. What better trends could anyone want for this particular day of the year? Even if you don't feel very much like working, when it comes to enjoying yourself the sky is the limit. Virgo can be as bright as the fireworks tonight, and just as wonderful!

RISING SIGNS FOR VIRGO

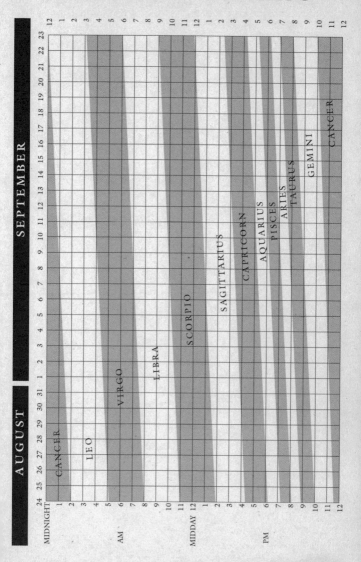

THE ZODIAC, PLANETS AND CORRESPONDENCES

The Earth revolves around the Sun once every calendar year, so when viewed from Earth the Sun appears in a different part of the sky as the year progresses. In astrology, these parts of the sky are divided into the signs of the zodiac and this means that the signs are organised in a circle. The circle begins with Aries and ends with Pisces.

Taking the zodiac sign as a starting point, astrologers then work with all the positions of planets, stars and many other factors to calculate horoscopes and birth charts and tell us what the stars have in store for us.

The table below shows the planets and Elements for each of the signs of the zodiac. Each sign belongs to one of the four Elements: Fire, Air, Earth or Water. Fire signs are creative and enthusiastic; Air signs are mentally active and thoughtful; Earth signs are constructive and practical; Water signs are emotional and have strong feelings.

It also shows the metals and gemstones associated with, or corresponding with, each sign. The correspondence is made when a metal or stone possesses properties that are held in common with a particular sign of the zodiac.

Finally, the table shows the opposite of each star sign – this is the opposite sign in the astrological circle.

Placed	Sign	Symbol	Element	Planet	Metal	Stone	Opposite
1	Aries	Ram	Fire	Mars	Iron	Bloodstone	Libra
2	Taurus	Bull	Earth	Venus	Copper	Sapphire	Scorpio
3	Gemini	Twins	Air	Mercury	Mercury	Tiger's Eye	Sagittarius
4	Cancer	Crab	Water	Moon	Silver	Pearl	Capricorn
5	Leo	Lion	Fire	Sun	Gold	Ruby	Aquarius
6	Virgo	Maiden	Earth	Mercury	Mercury	Sardonyx	Pisces
7	Libra	Scales	Air	Venus	Copper	Sapphire	Aries
8	Scorpio	Scorpion	Water	Pluto	Plutonium	Jasper	Taurus
9	Sagittarius	Archer	Fire	Jupiter	Tin	Topaz	Gemini
10	Capricorn	Goat	Earth	Saturn	Lead	Black Onyx	Cancer
11	Aquarius	Waterbearer	Air	Uranus	Uranium	Amethyst	Leo
12	Pisces	Fishes	Water	Neptune	Tin	Moonstone	Virgo